Maid (less) in India

SECOND EDITION

By

RITU GUPTA

PEEPEE
Publishers and Distributors (P) Ltd.

Published by:
Pawaninder P. Vij & Anupam Vij
Peepee Publishers and Distributors (P) Ltd.
Head Office: 160, Shakti Vihar, Pitam Pura
New Delhi-110 034

Correspondence Address:

7/31, Ansari Road, Daryaganj
New Delhi-110002 (India)

Ph: 65195868, 23246245, 9811156083

e-mail: **peepee160@yahoo.co.in**

e-mail: **peepee160@rediffmail.com**

e-mail: **peepee160@gmail.com**

www.peepeepub.com

Author Note

Second Edition: 2018

ISBN: 978-81-8445-236-5

About the Author

Ritu Gupta, is a management graduate from Indian Institute of Management, Bangalore and Gold Medalist from Delhi University, and is currently living in Delhi, India. Having worked as an Insurance Domain Specialist in the IT sector for almost 25 years, she recently moved out of the corporate world to lead a domesticated life pursuing her interests including writing. Having a strong sense of humor, she enjoys laughing at day-to-day problems that one faces in the normal course of life, especially her own. This book is an attempt at sharing some of her personal experiences, as well as those of her acquaintances, around the maid horror stories in India.

This book is dedicated to all my comrades in anguish, who are enduring the countless tortures meted out to them by the most important member of their households...their maids.

Preface

Maids….. whimsy superwomen (who if ever existed with the aspired qualities would have conquered Indian hearts and ruled Indian households forever; well the latter they anyway do) are the backbone of every middle class family in India. Anyone having stayed in an Indian house for a very short duration would have seen what trials and tribulations an Indian woman goes through juggling between multiple roles, hoping and praying to one day achieve a constant in her continuously changing maid universe.

Besides providing a stable (?) support system, these whimsical girls and ladies also perform a very important function…. Gossip material…. They are the favorite gossip topic, not only amongst women but even amongst some men and kids! Each household, each neighborhood, each social structure has an abundance of maid stories. Why? Because dealing with them is a daily struggle! Each woman (and some men) has her own treasure box of the learnings that each new maid has given her; or rather I should say continues to give her on a periodic basis.

I have always found it amusing how these girls and women, who are employed for making our lives easier, create a complexity in our lives that we wouldn't have thought of! Even when dealing with the biggest challenges with maids, I have found myself distancing myself from the situation and having a good laugh at the emotions and strategies that are at play.

So one day I decided to start jotting down some of these experiences, (mine and others) and the associated emotions enveloping the same. With an almost eighteen-hour, back breaking, daily schedule of office and home responsibilities, I lost the enthusiasm quite early on. To motivate me, my brother in law, Rajat Jain, jumped in to write some of his and his acquaintances' experiences. Suddenly we realized that between the two of us, we have written quite an interesting set of anecdotes.

When my sisters and I started reading this assortment of experiences, we could not stop laughing. Just when we were having a good laugh, I received a call from a wailing cousin, exhorting me for help in a new maid search. After giving her assurances, I started sharing these anecdotes with her. She immediately calmed down. During the next few days, I realized that what Rajat and I had collected was possibly a treasure house. So I decided to develop a storyline around these anecdotes and publish it. Rajat was very excited about it, as were my two daughters, Mansi and Manvi. In fact, Mansi wrote down one additional anecdote for my intended book. My first attempt was still a simple motley of experiences. After a couple of reviews with Rajat and my two sisters, Nidhi Singhal and Prachi Jain, I was able to construct a structure and storyline to share these day-to-day trials of most Indian women. I am sure every woman; and some men (the married ones at least!) would relate to this quite poignantly. It's all about my (and every woman's) day to day maid troubles.

Acknowledgements

I would like to express my heartfelt gratitude to my brother in law Rajat Jain, without whom this book would not have been possible.

I would also like to thank my family and friends who shared with me their maid experiences and associated adrenaline flows. I would like to thank my sisters, Nidhi and Prachi, who provided support, talked things over, read and offered comments. They and my daughter, Mansi, were the final editors for my book.

I would also want to thank my daughters, Mansi and Manvi, and my husband Sunil, who continually supported and encouraged me to take this up when I was getting cold feet.

A special thanks to my niece and nephew, Niharika Gupta and Gaurang Agarwal along with Mansi, for helping me develop and implement the initial promotion strategy around this book.

Contents

Disaster Strikes

My world had fallen apart….I could not believe it! She had simply walked out on me……..How could she, how could she do this to me! We had shared some of the most beautiful moments of our lives together. She had been at my side through good times and bad.

…..Always my closest friend and confidant. Why was this happening to me! I couldn't bear the pain and the desolation!

The day had begun beautifully, though as I reminisce, I did remember a weird feeling in the morning that sort of warned me of impending disaster, but such is life and its travails.

As stated, it had felt like a very good morning, the breeze was gentle and I could hear the chirping of the birds in my balcony. I had felt rejuvenated by the warm sun rays, filtered by the leaves of the nearby tree, not too warm, not too cold, just right, brushing my skin as it seemed to climb up, slowly increasing its intensity for the day. I could see the sky was clear.

If only I could get a cup of *masala chai*, I had yearned! But was not worried, as I was sure that later, once I have finished my daily routine, I would get one in peace. But, alas! It was not meant to be, as I had just found out.

As usual, I was packing our lunches for the office, when I noticed that a frightfully expensive cake that I had bought for that day's dinner had been reduced to a morsel. Perplexed, all I did was ask her if she knew what had happened to it. That's all, a simple question. All hell broke loose thereafter.

Mehak, my 14 year old, mentioned she had seen Kantabai helping herself and polishing off a wholesome piece. Before I could speak Kantabai started shouting and crying, stating that we always accuse her for anything that goes missing, she cannot live with this kind of distrust.

"So what if I have taken a piece of the cake, am I not part of the family, everyone is entitled to some benefits and rights, don't you think so?"

And before I could utter a word she dropped her bomb….. *"Bhabhiji, I'm leaving, am going and packing my stuff right away, please keep my wages ready!"* and she walked off.

I kept trying to plead with her, to at least have a dialogue; but couldn't get a word through in between her continuous rambling. I knew from past experience that there is no going back, she would not stay. Yet, hoping against hope, I pleaded with her, I promised to increase her wages but she was adamant.

"No, Bhabhiji, enough is enough, I cannot take this kind of insult. How can this little chit of a girl (pointing to Mehak) spy over me!!"

I looked at Mehak pleadingly; conveying my distress with my eyes, beseeching her to apologize to Kantabai, but that indeed was too much to expect; a teenager apologizing to a maid because she had caught the maid red-handed!

I tried to hold on to her under another camouflage; *"You still owe me 1000 rupees from the last advance over and above this month's wages so I am not giving you a penny. You'll have to return the 1000 rupees before I can let you go."*

She promptly took the money out and gave it to me. I was aghast; all my tricks were turning out to be ineffective. Interestingly, just previous night she had pleaded with me that she desperately needed 200 bucks as she had to buy some clothes and she had already send all her own money home!

Anyway, no point in bringing that up now, it wouldn't make her stay back! So, I had to let her go. The catastrophe had struck. I knew I should not give in to despair as I veered towards the 'no maid' scenario.

I looked around, the house was a mess. Muskan, my seven year old, had left her paintings strewn all over the place. The paint marks on the ground did not make it any better, and a sense of despondency started to creep in. I had almost started breaking down. But then I realized it was past 7 am, and my kids van was expected any moment. Before attending to the vibrant landscape I needed to send my kids to school. Quickly I packed them off and sat down to gather my breath, or what was left of it.

That's when it hit me! *Oh my God!! I am without a maid. No one is going to clean my house; no one is going to make tea for me when I come from office, no one to attend to my kids when they come home. OH MY GOD!! I have to go through this all over again; the hunt for a suitable maid needs to start RIGHT NOW!* And then I howled. I howled as if my heart would burst open, I cried as if this was the end of the world for me; which in a way it was.

I remembered a mail chain that I had read a few days back and laughed at "Women in India die of two things; one if they have – AIDS, other if they do not have – MAIDS" but this time I could not laugh at it.

I wailed even more loudly. Sameer knew trying to console me would lead to BIG quarrels. Nothing he could say, nothing whatsoever, would comfort me. He knew its best for him to keep out of it at that moment. May be after a couple of days when I was a little more amenable to listen, will he come up with suggestions. Till then, the best way to comfort me was to start finishing some of the tasks left unattended, quietly, in other rooms and kitchen.

Missing Address

Since, my mother in law's household, and her temper were heavily dependent on ready availability of good maids, my father in law used to keep collecting information on maid agencies, a treasure box that could be dipped into in the hour of need. This definitely was that hour for me.

He gave me a visiting card of an agency in the heart of the city that had been dropped at their gate a few days back. *Very professional looking card*; this got me excited that maybe this one would have some good smart girls who could fill the void in my life.

So I made the call.

"Yes, Ma'am, we will have all types of maids available; trained, semi trained, untrained in a week's time."

"Wow! What time can I come and pick one up."

"I would be visiting your area this Sunday, with a maid that I am providing to another household, so I can bring one for you as well. Will that work for you Madam?"

"Sure! I mean, yes, this will definitely work, please come on Sunday."

In my joy, I forgot to ask about the cost and other details. I was thrilled. I immediately called Sameer to share with him this exhilarating news!!

Sameer, being a typical level-headed, practical Taurean, stated we should pick the girl up ourselves, so that we can see the whereabouts of the agency, and also be in a position to choose from the maids available. Anyway, we were going to that part of the city that Saturday, for a friend's house warming party. Hence, we decided we will check with the agency and pick the girl up ourselves.

The ensuing week was a week of exhilaration! Everyone around me was happy with the buzz that I generated. My colleagues, my family, my friends; all commented on how cheerful and happy I looked. Umpteen times, I was caught daydreaming, I was about to graduate from a part time maid scenario to a full time one, I was about to climb the ladder of success, what a feeling. I couldn't stop myself from visualizing the luxury of having someone at my service when I reached home, dead tired after an eventful meeting; the luxury of getting up at 6:30 AM instead of 5 AM as there would be someone preparing the meals; what a bliss!!

Saturday came and we had to get ready to go to the friend's. I had never been more excited.

"Wow, someone is eager to go", Sameer commented, *"You seem to be the first one to get ready for this occasion; a rare occurrence."* No guesses for the reason behind it!!

Once we reached the party, I could hardly wait for the party to end. I kept watching Sameer's drink, which today seemed to be a never ending affair!! On top of it, he was busy chatting with the hostess. I was getting restless. Meanwhile, when the banter was over, ladies were back to discussing their favorite topic, maids! I was becoming increasingly uncomfortable as I was without one, and though I was on the verge of getting one, the wait was getting painful and unbearable by the minute. I pulled Sameer in a corner and CLEARLY INSTRUCTED him that as soon as we could excuse ourselves, without being rude, I would like to move out, so he had better have his food before that.

He sobered down immediately, quickly gobbled in his food and we were soon out on the road. Such excitement! The search for the address began.

First, finding the apartments was a challenge and then the apartment number seemed to have disappeared. After going around helter-skelter for over an hour, we finally found the address in the small by-lanes.

With great anticipation, Sameer and I climbed up the stairs to the fourth floor and rang the bell. The lady who opened the door looked really tired and unhappy. Feeling sorry for her, I asked in a polite tone;

"Hello, is Mahesh available right now?"

"Who Mahesh, there is no one by that name!"

"Isn't this the 'Mangalam Placement Agency'?

"What Agency? This is no agency. So many times I've told people this is my house; humble house but mine. Someone should complain about this Mahesh, whoever he is. Why has he given my number! If I get my hands on him, I'll bash him up ......" exclaimed the lady! And she slammed the door on our face.

For a fraction of a second there was darkness all around me, I thought I was fainting. But then Sameer nudged me and brought me back to consciousness. We rang the bell again and apologized to the lady and with a heavy heart started climbing down.

Once inside the car it struck me; *Oh my God!! We had been fooled!! If Sameer hadn't had the foresight to go and fetch the maid on our own, we would have been duped!!* I recalled how some of my friends who had taken maids from agencies could not locate the agency after the maid ran away; even where they had personally gone to the agency and picked up the maids. I was furious! I had to get this guy caught. I told Sameer that we should report this to the police. I mean, not every woman has such a wise husband!

So many women in agony would be getting duped and distressed because of such unscrupulous characters. The least I would do was expose the ones I encounter. But again my practical husband brought me back to my senses. *"Look dear, you do have limited time. What would you prefer to utilize it in; getting these goons caught or finding your maid?"* I realized I needed to prioritize. So I gave up the idea of lodging an immediate FIR and went back home, empty handed and momentarily defeated….

Mission Maid

Next day, I took up the challenge, I shall not be defeated. I took a day off from work and went on a mission - "Mission Maid". A neighbor had advised me that there were many agencies near our place and if I went hunting I should get someone. So after checking again with my agent about the availability of a replacement, I went to this area known to be a stomping ground of maid agencies. I started with the ones visibly located on main road with zero success. Then someone told me that there were agents who can be approached from the by-lanes.

A wave of terror gripped me when I saw the buildings that needed to be explored! .....Shady, dark, pretty wanton area....*Should I take the risk?*

Can I afford to abandon the mission? Questions flashed in my mind...*which is a bigger danger; agonizing days without a maid or these dingy but crowded areas?* Well, I had removed my jewelry before venturing on this mission, plus I had hardly any cash in my handbag. So there really was not much that could go wrong. I took a grip on my emotions and told my cab driver which building I was starting my exploration with. I instructed him that if I do not come down in 10-15 minutes, he had to come up. He should watch over and check that I continue to move from one building to another. This seemed almost like coming out of a spy novel or a movie!

Walking up the stairs I saw a crowd of young ladies doing household work. I was quite optimistic that one of them could well be the light of my life. On reaching the agency office, I enquired excitedly about the availability of a maid. I mean, I had seen so many of these ladies along the way that I was sure; he would have someone for my needs. Perceiving my desperation, he quoted an obnoxiously high price. I was stunned and screamed, *"Bhaiya, that's outrageous!! I have been paying almost a third of it."* I bluffed, *"I mean, 20-25% more commission I can understand but three times?"* He promptly replied, *"Madam, the risks that we take to bring these ladies to the city are enormous. Out of every three girls who start from the villages, just about one reaches us. The police harassment, their weekly bribe and administrative expenses are over and above this. I can give you a discount of 10% but that's about it!"* Well, that was it; I still hadn't reached a stage of complete despair.

Another reference was promising to give me someone in a couple of days, and then there were these other agencies that I had to try out. So with a heavy heart, I moved out of this first building.

I walked from one agent to another for almost 4-5 hours but my "Mission Maid" failed completely. It wasn't that they didn't have any maids, but either they looked real dumb; who could hardly comprehend my questions or were over smart; having demands like I would not enter the kitchen when they were in there!! Anyway, my five grueling hours lead to a naught.

Looking at all these young, seemingly unaware, girls reminded me of my sojourn with my maid previous to Kantabai. She had been sacked after she got pregnant, (apparently an affair with a construction worker gone wrong…). There was apparently nothing wrong with her. In fact, she was quite good at her work, and did not seem to have many distractions. She kept herself clean and was also good with the kids. But getting pregnant was definitely quite a distraction.

Later, I had recollected, she used to talk quite a bit on her mobile phone. Maybe that is what got her in trouble in the first place. It all started when some construction started in the neighbor's house.

The contractor and the workers used to come regularly and interact with her on the pretext of drinking water. Harmless indeed! Following the policy of help thy neighbor, our maid went all the way, maybe a little too much. They exchanged numbers, maybe fixed up a time for a quickie, probably without the necessary protection.

She had her sojourns in the loneliness of the park behind our house, inside the abandoned stone hutment. Much to my horror, I found out, this was made possible by our not so high balcony, which she could conveniently jump out of, with the help of the branch of a blasted tree. These branches had been encroaching into our house for ages, but due to the famed bureaucracy of the civic bodies, we could not get the requisite permissions and these could not be trimmed.

She had been twelve weeks pregnant when I learnt of her state and I called her paramour. He accepted his contribution (thank God!) and during the discussion that ensued, the man gave her a pill, which she just popped in. She said she would be okay by next day and was willing to continue. However, I fired her and sent her packing with the agent immediately as I did not want to take any risks in the future.

Coming back to the gloomy present, on my way back, I called Sameer and bawled all over again. He promised to come home early and take me out for shopping and a nice cozy meal. When I reached home, Mehak immediately got me some juice; looked like she had been pre-warned about my mental state and had been instructed to take care of me. Muskan too came and hugged me and started relating funny anecdotes from her school.

Finally, a few days later, out of nowhere, while laboring with household chores after a grueling day at office, I got the much awaited call.

"Madam, I heard that you require help?"

Now what kind of a question is that? Indeed, I do require a lot of help. And with this call my karma changed and I found my next "live-in" maid.

Mamta was a young girl of 22, whose sister Khushi was working nearby. Mamta too had worked earlier in a household close to my place but since the couple had left for another city few months back, she had gone home. She was married and had a kid who stayed with her husband in the village. When I asked her why she had not taken up another work immediately, she said she wanted a sabbatical before she joined a new household to be able to take the earlier household out of her system.

I remember thinking what luxury! I mean, I can't imagine leaving my job for a few months and then expecting to get an equally good or even better job.

What she did during that sabbatical, I thought, was none of my business. If there was any untoward activities, I guessed, police verification would uncover it (which Sameer told me was a stupid expectation as he had his reservations on the veracity of these police verifications, which I always insisted on for every new house-worker). Anyway, her story was that she had gone to meet her husband and child in the village but had come early as the village life was too dull. *Dull?*

*Hmm...maybe, I should reconsider....*But then I observed, she was appropriately dressed and was not much of talker and seemed perfect for the job. I hired her right away.

Mamta was everything I could ask for in a maid. Best was that my kids took to her like fish takes to water. I would not say she was perfect, but it wasn't perfection that I was seeking, my need was for efficiency. And this girl did turn out to be really efficient.

Being Maid-less Again

A year later…and the weather changes.

The weather was slightly overcast if not cloudy and it looked like an interesting Monday afternoon. I could see the trees swaying around and I thought of switching on some soft music on my phone, when a reminder alerted me that it was time for coffee. What a great weather to start the week, I mused, watching from my cabin on the top floor. Actually, it was the recent news that had lifted my spirits to the extent that everything looked so bright and beautiful!

"Congratulations! Rashi, you are being promoted to the position of a VP! Your brilliant performance and indomitable spirit has resulted in you being the youngest VP in the organization! Congrats once again."

Yippee! I feel on top of the world, is what I thought! Vikas had given me the best news for the day, sorry year, and I had entered my cabin with an elated spirit. I immediately messaged Sameer, who was in Tokyo, and prompt came the reply, *"We will celebrate it with a grand party once I am back."*

Yeah, I have made it. I would indeed like a wonderful celebration. Feeling on stage, as if I was taking the Miss India award (or rather Mrs. India award), I felt like thanking all those who made it possible. Putting a reign to my vivid imagination, I mentally started ticking off all the to-dos that needed to be taken care of for my celebration;

a) Prior engagement – Check No

b) Kids homework – Would get done on Friday itself

c) Kids bed time –Mamta will take care

Letting my guard down, I continued my day-dreaming.

*Friends coming over for dinner over the week end, the compliments and celebration, the entire weekend menu…..*when the coffee, that I had asked Amrita to get, arrived,

"Thanks Amrita, you are indeed a savior!"

Sipping the hot coffee, leaning against my favorite wall along the window, I stepped back to savor the moment. This cabin was the result of years of hard work that I had put in. The cabin itself was sparsely decorated but I made sure it carried my qualifications and some awards mounted on the walls.

I started feeling a slight pressure for the buildup over the next few weeks. I wanted to begin right away and plan ahead with new business plans, to align my team. There was so much to do….

And then around 5 PM, the phone rang!

"Mummy! Mamta Didi is missing!" Mehak screamed into the phone. *"She has not returned since 2."*

"What do you mean, missing?"

"I haven't seen her since 2, since the time Muskan and I went to watch TV in our room. I came out to ask for a snack but could not find her, so I have called you."

The color drained from my face! All the elation and joy of the last few minutes evaporated quickly to be replaced by the fear of being MAIDLESS again in this bad mad world. I sat down feeling totally defeated.

For a woman, being maid-less is the biggest nightmare! There is this old joke in our family that if I see my husband and my maid walking down from two different directions, after a week of absence, I would rush to welcome the maid first. My joy, and hence, the welcome that my husband would receive, would pale in comparison to what would be meted out to the maid.

How self-preservation takes precedence over all emotions! The transformation from a successful corporate woman to a miserable maid-less home-maker happened so quickly; that it would have been funny had it not been tragic! Thankfully, no one was around to witness the transformation.

How can this be happening to me again? What have I done to deserve this? The clouds had started to turn grey and it felt as if it was going to rain. *Sometimes, the weather plays tricks, starts off on a promising note but ends up with a lousy scare, or is it just me?* I wondered.

How I had thought this was my lucky day, instead what a disaster it was turning out to be!! All my best laid plans came crashing down. *Crash, boom, bang!* I could hear the crockery getting smashed with no maid to clean it up! Oh! My imagination again started to run wild!

Control!

Maybe I am worrying too much. Over reacting, Sameer says, is my habit. Maybe she has just gone to her sister's place which is not too far off...but walking off without a trace, that's unlike Mamta. But hey, anything can happen......

I called up Sameer;

"Hello! Yes Rashi?"

"Sameer, Mamta is gone."

"Rashi, just a minute... Hey congrats on your promotion, did you say something about Mamta? Can this wait, can we talk later? I am in the middle of a formal dinner and I cannot talk for long."

"Sameer, Mamta has gone missing! Mehak called up and she has not returned home for the past 3 hours. This is an emergency; you take some time out from your goddamn dinner and let us talk. I don't know what to do?"

"Aren't you overreacting? Mamta should be back soon, she cannot just walk away, there has to be some sane explanation to all this. Anyway, Rashi, I cannot skip this, I will call you as soon as I get free. Please manage this...OK? Will call you later and congratulations on your promotion once again. Bye."

What!! Manage this? What does he mean by saying this? I have to manage and he has no responsibility? I feel as if I am the one who is responsible for everything, juggling all the balls, and all the others, including Sameer, are just living in a hotel. Everything around me was falling like a pack of cards. Mentally shaking myself I reprimanded; *"Hey Rashi, get a grip girl!"*

I started to make some phone calls. The first call went to Mamta's sister.

"Khushi?"

"Yes Madam?"

"Has Mamta come over to your place?"

"No Madam, what happened?"

"She has left the house and has not come back. Do you know where she could be?"

"No Madam..." and then silence, and the call got over. No sign of Mamta.

She had not heard from Mamta and I released she too had got scared when I told her that her sister is missing. Woman safety was a precious commodity in the city these days and a young girl, out there alone, was a dangerous proposition.

Next I called up home.

"Mehak?"

"Yes Mamma?"

"I want you to do the following; lock the front door and do not open it till I arrive, not for anyone, not even for Mamta didi, is this ok?"

"Yes Mamma, by the way can I have some cookies and chocolate from the fridge? I will also give to Muskan."

"Yes Mehak, you can have them. And I repeat, do not open the door for anyone, ok?

"Yes Mamma, understood, you don't need to repeat. Bye."

I then stuffed my bag, called up Amrita to cancel my appointments, called Vikas to inform that I am leaving early because of MAID CRISIS and promised to call him after reaching home and taking stock of the situation.

Ok done. Now head for home.

Face the goddamn traffic! And keeping with my mood, it started to rain! I had forgotten to bring any umbrella; *lady luck has really abandoned me today!* I pulled out my car from the office complex into the sea of vehicles, all probably wanting to go back home.

Oh God, what a traffic! Has everyone's maid gone missing today? How come everyone is out on the road at exactly the same time?? People are standing, with their two wheelers, under the bridges and shades, blocking the sides, the roads are water clogged and mini rivulets can be seen on the side! How does one hope to reach home! Oh god, help me! This is going to be a long haul.

I still remember the day; Mamta had come to our house about a year back. I had personally cleaned up the house so that the house did not look too dirty. She surveyed the house, with an expert eye and had agreed.

As Mr. Olivander told young Harry Potter, “wands choose wizards”, well in today’s world maids choose employers! They are very quick in their decision making and extremely perceptive about assessing the amount of work which they will be required to do in a day.

It is easier managing your top performers and a team of 200 people with their aspirations, salaries, perks, and get them to work as an A Team, than to manage the complexities associated with these maids.

I then started to think about Bina. She was the ideal help and stayed with us for 5 years…..

Old Maid: Fond Remembrance Long Years, Then…

"B*reakfast, madam, hope the milk temperature is Okay."*

"Yes, Bina, as always!"

"Did Mehak create a fuss while going?"

"No Madam, she was good. The driver was asking for this month's bus fees." I told her to remind me the next morning before the kids leave.

"Madam, here is the list of grocery items that I need for the house." It was a luxury that I did not have to bother about maintaining stock of groceries, vegetables and other routine household items.

"Ok, Bina, I will order them online and they will deliver these by evening. You can check and call me to confirm, ok? Also don't make dinner; I will get something interesting to eat for all of us."

Those were the times! When the roads were less crazy, life was more organized and the office space was under construction, with just a few people having moved in. At office, we were finding our feet and trying to make various business models work; while at home, I was safe and secure. At that time, I did not walk past those groups of young people making plans for the evening; I used to be the one making them!

Bina was the lord and master of our house. She was married and had come to the city for work. She wanted to buy back her house and land in her village and hence she was saving everything for her goal. She was focused and extremely efficient.

Bina had joined us days before my sister's wedding. The entire wedding celebrations were in the week following her arrival and there were multiple things to be done. Mehak was less than a year old and the regular maid had run out on me, leaving town (supposedly) for good. She had left us in a lurch.

Bina and I were simply made for each other. We both had been desperate and maybe that's why destiny brought us together. She was introduced to me by one of my part timers. She needed work and I wanted to keep someone desperately. She handled Mehak very well during the wedding, helped take the responsibility off me, so that I could focus on the festivities.

But good maids also have their idiosyncrasies, and I saw them emerge gradually, once she got comfortable in our house. A standing joke in my household was that the moment we got whiff of someone coming to stay with us, we knew Bina is going to get her migraine attack! Without fail, a day before the guest's arrival one could witness Bina's forehead wrapped up in a piece of cloth and soon not show up for work till they left. Anyway, since these were temporary phases, I overlooked this trait.

She took care of my Mehak as her own; as she herself did not have any kids yet. She managed the groceries, cleanliness and, even to a large extent, the health of our family, as she promoted healthy eating habits. Everyone in the house listened to her suggestions.

She worked with me for five years and as a farewell gift, we gave her a bank account with a fixed deposit in her name, which would mature after five years. I also bought her a life insurance policy linked to her bank account, with part premium paid. For the rest, she just needed to ensure money in her bank account and it was to be automatically debited. She saved enough and had bought back her land. We also gave her many gifts for her new home. Ah, she was an angel! But she was not coming back…..

Present Day – Maid Crisis Continues

What is the elixir of woman's life? A reliable maid; an elusive dream! A woman can live without a husband but cannot survive a day without the domestic help.

Honk! Honk! Siren! *Hey Lady, move! Don't hold up the traffic.* I had started to hear some voices, now what's the matter?

Suddenly, I realized that I was in the middle of a traffic jam and saw a traffic policeman starting to walk towards me.

"Madam, you are blocking the way, is there a problem? If so, can you pull to the side."

"No officer, there is no problem, just dozed off I guess!"

"Are you not well?"

"No I am okay, thanks, I will move now." I quickly pulled my car away and lost myself into the midst of the cars in the front.

What has happened to Mamta? Where is she? Why did she leave? What do I do now?

Finally, after riding the puddles and making my way across the rivulets, I reached home. As I got out of my car, another vehicle came zipping past me and splashed the muddy water across my dress and face. *Could this get worse?* I picked up my bag and reached home…….legs and mind aching due to a heady cocktail of brakes, clutch, and some mini stretches of accelerator during the drive. I rang the bell, even though I had my keys, to check what would be Mehak's reaction.

"Who is it? Oh Mummy.....Ok.". Mehak opened the door, after the usual due diligence of name check and face recognition through the keyhole. I was relieved.

She went back to her room, a bit apprehensive, but without a care in the world. The kids were watching TV, as usual. Maybe, kids are better suited to such situations than adults.

I went and poured myself a glass of cold water .... Normally, Mamta used to bring it for me! Small luxuries.....I think I need stronger stuff, but for the moment water had to suffice. Taking deep breaths to calm myself, I sat down to think. *What could have happened?* Mamta used to have a corner where she kept her things; hence I started to look into Mamta's belongings for any clues or phone numbers....nothing. I took a piece of paper and started to note down all the contacts that Mamta ever had.

I called up Sanam, who had given her reference and claimed to be her friend. Sanam was also clueless...She gave me some more numbers and I called them up, no clue came forward. One call led to another and after a number of calls, I managed to reach her family, but they too had no clue. Now, I was scared. I was getting more and more anxious. Just then Sameer, called up.

"Rashi, are the kids ok? What happened?"

I narrated the entire incident. No reply!
"Sameer, when can you come back?"

"Back? Rashi, I have meetings till Thursday, and the earliest, I can arrive is by Friday morning...please try to manage..."

Hmm...Sameer is of no use till the end of the week, I thought, *so let me see.*

I called up my mother. She stayed in another city and had a very busy social life. She was always busy organizing get togethers, health camps, short duration trips and similar events for the senior citizens in her area. She was also quite knowledgeable when it came to the subject of maids. She listened patiently to my plight and told me to report the matter to the local police station.

"Police! Mummy are you kidding? I have never visited a police station."

"Beta, I think it cannot be avoided this time"

"Oh, trust my luck, now I will have to go to the police station."

She asked me if I had seen or heard anything amiss in the last week. After much thinking, I remembered a young man had come to our house, one Sunday, when Mamta had gone to Sanam's place, asking for her.

I had replied in the negative and had enquired about who he was.

He had mentioned to just inform Mamta that a guy came looking for her and she would understand. He also said he would come again. When I conveyed the message to

Mamta, she did not say anything. I had dismissed this event as a one off. But now I was worried even more.

In case something happened to Mamta, police would come looking; hence it was better to inform them proactively. I realized mummy was right, as always, and I needed to file a report at the local police station. Meanwhile, she comforted me stating that there was nothing to worry about; things would automatically take care of themselves. She had some urgent things to take care of and hence she called off, promising to call in a couple of days to check.

I started to have a sinking feeling in my heart, I had never visited a police station in my life, and now I had to grapple with this horror, along with the pending household chores.

Anyway, I put together a snack for myself, took a shower, and with the kids in tow; I reached the local police station. It was just a five minute drive from our house but I had never bothered about its existence until now. It was a red colored building, built in the old British style, and carried the police housing colony as well. The road was nicely paved and the parking was relatively empty. Its entrance was wide open and there was some commotion inside.

I parked my car and asked for the reporting section, and was asked to wait. At the waiting wooden bench, I jostled for space between two ladies, looking menacingly at each other. I managed to wedge between them and asked the kids to play close by.

The kids, oblivious of their surroundings were very excited; this was their "TRIP TO THE POLICE STATION". They were very excited to see so many policemen in one place. Muskan was scared as we sometimes used to threaten her that if she would be naughty, we would take her to the police station.

"Mummy, will they lock me up?"

"No Muskan, I am here for some work, just relax". They started to play loudly and I had a tough time controlling them. After waiting for half an hour, I managed to reach the reporting section. The room in which the concerned officer was sitting seemed right out of the movies. It had an old wooden desk, with the picture of Gandhi ji hanging on the wall behind him. There were some other police officers sitting but none were speaking anything. The old chair in which I sat was groaning, as if in pain. I took a few deep breaths, gathered myself and started to speak calmly.

The tall and menacing police officer in the reporting section was surprisingly quite polite. He asked me to describe the situation, which I did. He advised me not to report this so soon and wait for a couple of days, as she may return in sometime, but I insisted.

"Madam, these women, we know them well. She must have gone somewhere, must be a lover. Relax, she will come back, don't worry." But I was in no mood to listen. So he started using delaying tactics; he mentioned accusingly, that he doubts whether I had got the police verification done. When I presented him with all the papers (Thank God for Sameer's advice!) he tried to intimidate me with whole series of questions around people she met, places she would frequent etc. The questioning and cross-

questioning was so intense, I felt that I myself were a culprit. Furious, exhausted and exasperated!

I finally met a senior policeman who agreed to file my report. But he wanted me to write the entire episode down for him, which I did promptly.

As I walked toward the door, searching for my kids, I saw Muskan being carried by a big policeman under his arm and Mehak trudging along.

Oh no!! Why are my kids being arrested!! My crazy frustrated mind screamed in my head!! Suddenly I heard their laughter, and came to my senses. They had just been playing. Ashamed of my thoughts, I thanked the policeman and walked off. My excuse was that I was really tired.

I came back completely drained; kids obviously were excited, as they had loads of tales to tell at school next day. I told them to soften their constant chatter, it was getting really late and I had to fix up dinner and get them to sleep. I called up Vikas, and told him that I will be taking off for the next two days.

"But Rashi, there is an important meeting coming up with the client on Friday. We need to prepare and discuss this. I can't do this alone."

"Vikas, I will log in from home for some time, prepare the framework for the discussion and send it to you by tomorrow. We can discuss this later. I need some slack as I already have my hands full. My maid has decided to run off and I was sitting at the police station this whole evening, instead of planning for my promotion party!"

"What?"

"Yes, I am going through a rough patch, I mean, I had to file a police report for the missing person. What do you think?"

"Okay, okay, calm down, I will manage to hold fort, please try and log in from home and send me some preparatory stuff so that I can work on it. And if you need any help, please call. I will, meanwhile forward you some of the agency contacts that my wife has; it's her prized possession, bye". I could almost hear the wink that followed. Anyway, Vikas hurriedly kept the phone down.

After Vikas, I called up Amrita for rescheduling my appointments. Amrita took them down and assured that these will be taken care of.

"*Rashi, I hope you get over this mess, but is it that bad? I mean, can't someone take care of this at home? Is there an agency that you can call, who can take temporary control till you find one?"* Being a young single girl of 23, she was blissfully unaware of the maid crisis that pervades the existence of almost all married women.

"Wow Amrita! I wish it was that simple. Anyway, you have a brilliant idea, maybe you can start one such agency yourself and I will get you at least a dozen customers immediately. Please hold fort and let me know in case of any emergencies, okay?"

Poor child, she had little inkling into the household mess that I was into; I thought, sounding a bit condescending to my own self, *maybe her mother would have been more sympathetic.*

After dinner, I had a usual round of games with kids. Then I helped the kids change into their favorite night suits and put them to bed, but not before checking their homework and schoolbags. Once Muskan was asleep, Mehak came up to me and asked what had happened. I told her that Mamta Didi had some work and had gone. I also told her that she may never come back, and hence we have to prepare for a new maid. She was satisfied with the explanation and promised to be cooperative.

Reach Out

Meanwhile, I started chatting on WhatsApp with friends who were invited for the weekend dinner and explained my situation. They were most sympathetic and quickly suggested pot luck (everyone brings a dish) at my place. When I asked for some contacts for an agency or getting new maid, there was an eerie silence on the group. Soon I dozed off as the burden engulfed my entire being.

Wakey! Wakey! It is morning time. Phew, what a day I had, was it a nightmare?

5 AM: it was still dark, slowly one eye opened and then the other and the marathon started.

It was time to start pumping water in the tank, as the fresh supply would last for only an hour.

6:30 AM: I had to wake up the kids, freshen them up and get them ready for school. Muskan, created a fuss while dressing up as her uniform was not ironed, Mehak had forgotten to polish her shoes previous night.... there was a race against time to finish all the tasks like a Super Mario video game! A constant voice kept screaming in my head.

"Mamta or others, where are you?"

Exclusive tasks for Mummy like packing the tiffin and filling the water bottle were to be completed in the same time as these added responsibilities. I prayed to God that nothing stops working or requires maintenance work in the house, else getting it fixed will be another chore.

Fortunately, luck was on my side, the things chugged along smoothly.

AHA! BUS STOP! A happy hunting ground for information on maid contacts and maid gossip! This was where I could hope for some redemption.

"Morning Rashi, nice to see you after a long time, you look tired, long day, not enough sleep? Where is Mamta?" The women group seemed to be abuzz on seeing me at the stop.

"You bet, nice to see you ladies, but you know my maid ran away...."

"Oh really, (rolling their eyes) how did this happen?" and then everyone gathered to hear me narrate my mis-adventure. With everyone in rapt attention, I let my moment of depression and hence expression, run full steam and it gave me some sense of temporary mental relief. Like a street performer, who is at her peak performance, I managed to narrate an intensely interesting saga to the audience, who listened to me with fascination. I took them through my ordeal, starting from the devastating phone call right upto my adventure at the police station.

I walked back with more confidence than I had when I started off today.

You may think that there is only one obsession in my life, getting a good maid, but that's not really true. Whilst they do comprise a significant part in maintaining my sanity, I have a whole bunch of other things to keep me mentally stressed!!

Well, let me very briefly share who I am, and where I live. As you would have gathered by now I am a working professional, married with two kids; one being a teenager, with the associated challenges. My house is not too big, but not too small either. It has three rooms, a couple of bathrooms and balconies, beautifully furnished with hand-picked items that I have gathered over the years, with a small garden in the front. Just the right amount of space one needs to survive in the city (and to be cleaned up by the maid regularly).

I stay in a relatively green part of the city, have a city park behind my house, though mostly neglected by the local authorities, lined with the trees and plants which bloom in the spring. Sometimes during the rainy season, you can see parrots climbing into the holes in the bark of the trees.

The flip side is that it needs regular cleaning as the leaves and the droppings accumulate around the house. While getting domestic help is a problem, getting civic help is even more difficult and getting some civic sense in people is next to impossible.

I would have loved to go on walks in the park but for the encroachments by some of the neighbors! If they had not cordoned off a large part of the park for their private use, it would have been sufficiently big for kids to play in. But alas! Aggressive, uncivilized people do manage to rule the world!

The place with all its greenery has its fair share of insects and rodents. The colony management tries to do its bit but due to perpetual lack of funds, as many residents continuously forget to pay their dues, they are also helpless.

Most people have no idea what it takes to keep a region clean and healthy.

These folks do not hesitate while spending an exorbitant amount in a restaurant or a parlor, but they have challenge paying up for the municipal charges and welfare expenses. They do not realize that if a fraction of what they spend on doctors and medicines were spend on creating a hygienic environment in the society it would be more rewarding.

This lack of building maintenance results in greater work within the homes. We, at our individual level, need to prevent these impediments to healthy living, from entering our homes.

Anyway, to continue with my current predicament, as I walked towards my house, I felt the gentle breeze and it started having a soothing effect. But this peace was momentary, the reality dawned…There is a fair amount of wind and dust that blows in our city and a substantial amount of dust suspiciously finds its way into our house. *Oh God!! Who would do the cleaning today!!*

Then my mind started meandering around; I think it's a self-defense mechanism to stay sane! I started thinking about the various methods we have learnt in the last few years to avoid any unwanted interactions our maid may have. Our house constantly needs repairs, hence the foot soldiers like plumbers, electricians and painters keep visiting us frequently. Whilst calling them over and overseeing them are Sameer's department, keeping them away from the maid is mine.

As these days, the foot soldiers do not turn up for small repairs and charge an exorbitant amount, Sameer had started to explore the options of self-repair kits and had even resorted to carrying the small repairs himself, over the weekends. This had led to many (mis)adventures. Recollecting some of them always has me rolling on the floor.

Once, while hanging a picture frame, we needed a nail to be driven into the wall. Sameer, armed with his newly acquired weapon, the drill kit and safety glasses, started the activity with much fanfare. Both the kids watched him with great anticipation and I hung around apprehensively. And sure enough, he drilled the hole right through the wall, so nicely that it went across through to the neighbor's wall. A big check to repair the damages followed our deeply heartfelt apologies. The foreman later pleaded with me, not to let Sameer touch the drill again, but of course his ego couldn't let him agree with such nonsense. Refusing to believe that this was not a skill he is adorned with, Sameer always found a reason why that was the very last time he had messed up.

On another day, to repair a leak in the bathroom, Sameer had successfully managed to crack open the tap, leading to a pool of water in the house. Our entire stored water in the overhead tank was wasted and our bathroom became a swimming pool. We managed to block the tap and curtail the flow of water, till the plumber came and repaired it. It was a petty task but since it had turned into a desperate situation, we had to pay extra. Worse still, the onus of cleaning the house landed on me as my maid had been on leave. I often wondered which was a bigger evil, cleaning up after Sameer's disastrous attempts at self help or managing the distance between male maintenance staff and my maids.

Male Co-workers –Complications

We had not kept any drivers to prevent any unnecessary complications amongst driver and maid.

One of my friends, Alpana, had had a terrible experience because of this combination of house workers. I remember how upset Alpana was one day, when she called me up and shared that her maid was accusing the driver of forcing her to have a relationship with him and the drama that followed. Her immediate reaction was that of outrage, but before she gave vent to her anger, the maid starting narrating the entire episode. Interestingly, she had been going steady with the driver for a few months. But now she wanted out, the driver was not accepting it.

The maid was scared that if she had got pregnant, her brothers would kill her. Alpana's mother in law was insisting that Alpana should get the maid's checkup done. *"Poor child, let's take here to a doctor, who can examine and find out if she is pregnant"*, she had insisted. Alpana tried to tell this mother of three and grandmother of five, that before her next cycle there is nothing a doctor can find out, but her mother in law, in all her motherly compassion, wanted to check with a doctor right away.

Instead of arguing with her, Alpana decided to take her to a gynecologist in the neighborhood, and narrated the whole story to her. The doctor confirmed what Alpana had been saying, nothing could be establish at that point in time.

Meanwhile, Alpana confronted the driver for his impropriety but he simply refused to accept his guilt. In fact, he showed his mobile log, to prove how the girl had been harassing him by calling up at all hours of the day and night! Some of the messages that she had send were outright obscene. He claimed that he was willing to undergo any test to prove his innocence!!

When Alpana narrated to me the whole incident, I was aghast at her naivety. I told her she was lucky that the doctor did not call any of these activist organizations; else she would have been in real trouble.

Anyway, this incident was alarming enough for me to not want male and female co-workers at home. As of now, both Sameer and I drive our vehicles ourselves.

On my way back, I sounded out the security guard and the shop keeper nearby from whom I pick up groceries to be on the lookout for a replacement and send them to me for the rounds of interview. Carpet Bombing!

Job description was partially or fully trained. Anyone who knows cooking, cleaning, nanny services; could apply!

Just to elaborate, I am a simple person, used to my simple routine and small pleasures, and I like it that way. In case that peace or balance gets disturbed, I end up operating like a commando in hostile situations.

7:45 AM: *Ah, one major task has got over, Kids have gone to school!* I was already feeling totally drained!! So I fixed myself a cup of tea, to allow my adrenalin to start flowing. *Oh God, tea does have therapeutic effect ....*

Suddenly my reverie was broken by a shrill noise of doorbell. Who could it be? Every 10 minutes there seemed to be someone at the door; the barrage of providers seemed to be unending.....first it was our garbage collection van, then came the milk man, followed by the laundry man, car cleaner, newspaper boy…*why can't they all come together?*

As feared, post the visit to the bus-stop, wherein the complete narrative of the previous day had been dramatically presented to a group of gossip loving ladies; the news about my predicament had spread around, with everyone plugging their news to the informal system of Chinese whispers. Everyone wanted their exclusive insights, right from the horse's mouth.

"Madam, what happened to Mamta?"

"I don't know you tell me."

"Oh Madam, she was such a sweet girl, never heard her voice."

"Oh really!"

"She was so prompt in her work."

"Have you seen her with someone lately?"

"No madam. I heard that you had to go to the police station; it is a very scary thought. Madam. These police-wallas can be very pesky, you know. They turn up at odd times asking you extremely difficult questions. Madam, be careful. My brother is in the police, in case you need help, let me know."

Trying to take a quick bite and read bits of newspaper in between I listened and answered to some of these questions.

The first batch of hopefuls was not expected to start before 11 AM, so I logged into my laptop and started preparing for the all-important meeting on Friday. I managed to put together some information, before the bell rang again!

Interviews

The much-awaited moment came. The candidates started arriving after completing their daily commitments at other places. While laying out my terms, I was in parallel trying to figure out the appropriate salary and the current market rate; which obviously depends on the work, locality and the skill of the person. I asked them about their availability, work preferences and timings.

"What is your name?"

"Sajida"

"Where do you stay?"

"Next door"

"Next door! Where?"

"Next door Madam, I stay in your neighbor's garage with my family as my husband is a driver with them."

"Oh ok! I need someone to come in early at 6 AM and stay till 7 PM and manage the entire household work."

"Madam, I only cook and wash clothes, and I have only two time slots available. Moreover, as a policy, I do not work in one household. My husband wants me to come back before 5 PM; hence, the late hours won't work. If you have anything for these slots, let me know." When she saw my reluctance to accept her terms, she turned around and left, even before I could utter a word!

"Madam, I work only on the week days, not on the weekends, I need these weekly offs with my family as we usually go out somewhere. In case it is ok, please let me know."

"Madam, I can come over for cooking in the afternoon only. After that I will also cook my food and take a quick nap, before going to the next house, around 4 PM."

I also got several others, but most of them were available for short time-slots and/or willing to do only specific tasks. *May be my requirements are too stringent,* I wondered. *I probably need to divide the work between two maids and modify my job requirements.*

"Madam, are you looking for someone for the day?" I saw a plumpish maid at my doorstep.

"Yes, I am"

"My name is Dolly, and I stay just round the corner."

"Oh great do come in Dolly."

"Thanks, Madam."

"I was referred by Mrs. Gupta, who stays in the house on the corner. My husband is a driver there. I can manage to stay for the day, but cannot do a lot of physical work."

This looked like a perfect arrangement. I started to feel elated and made a mental note to thank Mrs. Gupta. As I was about to pop the inquiry of why she couldn't do any physical work, Dolly asked, "*Madam, can I use your toilet, I am not feeling well.*"

"Okay", and lo behold, without waiting for the answer, she went in and puked inside. It suddenly dawned on me that she was on the family way. I asked her, *"how many months?"*

"Am in my seventh month, my baby is due any time after one and a half months."

I weighed the odds; my desperation vs long term viability as she would at best be a short term arrangement, that too working under constrained conditions. I politely told her it wouldn't work.

Meanwhile the primary query that every prospect had was "*why did the previous maid leave*?" I had no clue, and I was forthright about it….

The first rounds of interviews were over and there was no one in sight. What a plight!

With no immediate relief, I had to start concentrating on how to accomplish household tasks, most importantly, some cooking, for lunch and maybe for dinner. Not to forget the dishwashing, laundry, cleaning and dusting of the house. Backbreaking work for someone not used to even half of it.

Just as I pulled up my sleeves and plunged into these activities, I was reminded of other activities I'd have to start myself in case no maid turns up; pest control, cupboard cleanup, RO cleanup, Ugh!! I am doomed. Not to forget the groceries and vegetables shopping. At this rate, I thought, I would be back in shape in a month's time, that is, if I could survive that month.

I Have Miles To Do, Before I "Can" Sleep!

I suddenly realized I had not done my daily treadmill, but who needed it that day. I was already sweating and possibly would have shed more calories than I could ever do with my daily sophisticated workout and diet control! *Shilpa Shetty and Jane Fonda, I bet if you do all this, and show it in your videos, it would become a super hit.* Going at that rate, I could have given them competition.

2:30 PM: It was time to go to the bus stop and pick up the kids. Anticipating the penetrating rays from the summer sun, I had quickly applied high SPF sun cream and had gone out to embrace the heat. As it started to get warmer and the moisture started to bite, the jumping jacks had arrived with all the energy of a bomb which is ready to explode.

Back home, the kids were finally out of their model behavior of school and started jumping up and down the house. Before I could manage to rein them in, they had spoiled the entire room which I had dusted just a few hours ago and my fuse was about to go BOOM! I took three deep breaths, after all nothing much had changed for them, instead of maid; they had a mother - simple!

"Mummy, I will not wear these clothes you kept on the bed, they are too tight."

"Why, we just bought them last month? What's wrong?"

"They are too tight and the weather is too sticky, I need loose clothes."

"Okay, just go and pick them."

"Great! You know mummy, didi never picked out our clothes, she just told us to change out of the uniform."

I was amazed; my maid had made my children self-reliant! I was so missing out on their growing up years. I would have to start paying more attention now.

"Also Mummy, the school tunic is tight; I need some new tunics".

I made a mental note to buy tunics over the weekend, if and when I reached there.

It's an ordeal to feed kids, since they are always so finicky. I had laid the food on the table and called out to them but there was no reply, no answer....so I called again.....no answer again....then I went into their room, I found the blaring TV! No wonder, they could not hear anything.....I switched it off and asked them to come over. With a dull face, they came and sat on the table.

"Mummy! I will not have this vegetable, I don't like this."

"Beta, you will have to have this. This is good for you."

"Oh, didi allowed us to eat in front of the TV", said Mehak.

Well, I do not allow kids to have meals with TV but that day I didn't have the energy to fight this battle, so I took them to their room, switched on their favorite channel and put their plates with the same meal in it. And they finished the whole plate!!

Strange.... Kids can eat anything when they are in front of the TV. I knew I could not allow it regularly, but I parked it for another day when I were more settled.

"By the way, Mummy, there are some circulars in the bag," Mehak came out for a second and then went back to her room. I saw them and marked my calendar for dates for PTM and quizzes, I sauntered off to my room for finishing my work for that Friday. I was so engrossed with the work that I just lost track of time, till my phone alarm reminded me about the kids' classes.

After "some" TV time (by my standard loads of it), it was time for them to go for their extra-curricular classes. I realized Muskan had dozed off on the bed and Mehak was watching some melodramatic family show. Getting Muskan up is always a challenge, attempted by only a rare breed of humans, as she creates such a ruckus that she can put a hurricane to shame.

"Muskan, get up baby, you need to go to you classes."

"I don't want to go."

"She says this everyday Mummy!"

"Mehak, you get up, pack your bag and get ready."

Muskan very reluctantly got up and went to the washroom. She packed her bag only when I gave her the incentive of some chocolate wafers in her snack box for the classes.

Again, they needed to be escorted to and fro for their classes. Meanwhile, on the way to the class, the inevitable happened….. "*Mummy, Muskan hit me!!"*

"Muskan why did you do that?"

"She was teasing me, so I just touched her, but she didn't have to hit me so hard."

"Mummy, Muskan hit me first."

"Ok...Ok...., now do not walk together, Muskan, you walk in the front."

Again, I heard grumblings…"*Mummy, Mehak is coming by the side and was about to overtake me."*

"I was just a step behind! Muskan is lying. Now I will also walk in front of Muskan."

"No Mummy, she cannot do this...." and it went on, as always. I had had it. I put my foot down, "*NO ONE is going to hit the other. If either of you is being teased, inform me and I would take the requisite action, but no fighting amongst each other! Is that understood?*" They both got the message loud and clear, though it took sometime for them to fall in line.

Back home, I managed to get some more inputs for the Friday meeting and then the exhaustion took over, so I just dozed off. Suddenly, I was woken up rudely by my phone. It was the sports teacher! *Oh dear, I had to pick up Mehak and Muskan fifteen minutes back from their sports class!!* I felt like a terrible mom!

"Mummy, why didn't you pick us up on time? I was scared having to sit alone when all the kids were gone." Feeling awfully guilty I mumbled, *"Sorry darling, I give you my pinky promise, this will never happen again"*.

They were really hungry too, so I gave them milk and evening snacks. Whilst attempting to do all the household tasks, I needed to ensure that my regular duties as a mother, also got done. So I started with their homework. *"Can both of you get your copies and your school bags?"*

I was exhausted, both physically and mentally, but there was no time to fret. As usual, some homework details were missing. *Oh! Why can't Muskan take down the complete homework!!*

So my usual savior, the WhatsApp group of parents, was invoked and pat came the reply from some helpful parent. Kids were put to work, and I got up to prepare dinner. After the dinner and some more TV watching, I packed the kids in their bed with a story, switched off the light and deliberated on the first day without maid, before I fell in a deep sleep.

I dreamt of a world where I was free from the challenges of daily living and had a day when I could just put up my feet, do and think of nothing....Pure bliss!!

By the time my alarm rang again, I had started to re-strategize and instead of one maid for all the work, I decided to keep two part-timers, or maybe one full time and another part timer. The idea seemed to grow on me as the day went by and I started calling....

Get Set Go

So I called up and appointed Sajida for the two tasks of cooking lunch and washing clothes, as per her availability. But the larger problem still continued to haunt me. Just as I was getting worried, I heard a rustle and the doorbell rang.

"Hello Madam, my name is Shanti." I saw a cheerful, bubbly, youngster, extremely eager for work.

"I have just arrived from the village and am presently staying at my aunt's place. I am looking for work and the reference was given by Mrs. Swami. My aunt works at her place and I thought I could apply."

"Hi Shanti, I need someone to manage the house, cleaning, dusting and other routine work. Lunch would be prepared by someone else but dinner would be this person's responsibility. Have you managed kids before?"

"Yes, I have younger siblings, in fact five of them, back home, and hence I can manage. I can come early morning and stay till 8 at night" She fit the bill pretty well so I hired her immediately.

With this, my plan to hire two part timers got accomplished. Shanti was to come early and remain at the house for the entire day. She would be responsible for all the household work except cooking lunch and washing clothes, which would be taken care of by Sajida. I asked them for their documents, photos, residence address proofs to fill the forms for the police verification (I NEVER take chances on this front!)

Next day onwards, my life started getting back to normal, well almost. When Shanti rang the bell at 6:30 AM, I had felt as if I am being lifted from a deep abyss, and the nervousness that I had been experiencing since previous night around the proverbial 'will she come (To be), will she not (or Not to be)' had evaporated. It seemed like I had a malady from which I had started to recover.

I also got a call from the local policeman asking me if he could visit that day to which I agreed. The local policeman came along with the reporting officer to whom I had narrated the entire story.

They listened patiently making their notes in the process.

"Madam, can you describe the person who came over on Sunday?"

I gave him the description to the best of my ability and recollect.

"Madam, is anything missing; money, jewelry, phone etc.?"

I replied in negative as I had already confirmed the same.

"Did she have any money with her when she left?"

Now this was something I had no idea about, I had not found any money amongst her belongings, which was strange, as she had taken her salary just a couple of days back. I informed the officer accordingly.

"Ah, so she could have gone on her own accord!"

There was a chance of that, but why she would leave all her other belongings here was something I could not comprehend! *Maybe, if she had taken all the things, it would have been too noticeable.*

As before, there was a lot of cross-examination, which again irritated me, but with the comfort of a maid, serving tea and snacks in the background, I managed to hold onto my temper. On hindsight, I believe it is their job, to make sure on the veracity of statements recorded. He took the necessary papers, photos and other details and promised to launch an investigation and keep me posted.

Meanwhile, I finished my work and sent that across to Vikas. With some back and forth deliberations the presentation was finalized. Vikas commented on how my thought process had matured with the crisis that I was handling. Made some comment around iron getting forged through difficulties. Teasing me he said that probably I should invite more such situations in my life, it would be good for the organization!

Friday morning! Day of my presentation….I was fully prepared and raring to go. Sameer called me from the Tokyo airport, wishing me luck …and I was upbeat. Mehak and Muskan had been dispatched to the bus stop and I had begun my daily routine with a 30 minute treadmill, a quick shower and a healthy snack, prescribed by my friend, who doubled up as my nutritionist.

After thanking the colony guard for extracting my car from our overcrowded and crazy parking, I managed the drive through the by lanes with skillful expertise honed over the years. Yes, a woman can drive very well, even on Delhi roads!

These lanes are inhabited by crazy, mindless drivers, who convert these roads to a racing track, deliberately simulating hazardous road conditions, making it a daily miracle for the normal commuters to reach their workplace in time, unscathed.

Arriving sharp at 8:55 AM, I parked my car at my marked slot in the building. It takes me around 5 minutes to reach my office from the car park. This designated slot is allocated to the top employees in our company. I was allocated this spot with the current promotion. Our company is one of the early ones in the building complex, which has now grown on to become one of the finest in the country. The buildings were designed on international standards and the who's who of business world vied for office space in this complex. The infrastructure and the revenue generated by this complex has become a benchmark.

With the growth anticipated in the economy, and business scenario looking upbeat, more and more businesses are setting up shop here. With so much business moving their offices to this complex, a whole set of entrepreneurs are setting up restaurants offering global cuisine at varying prices. With this, parking has become a bit of a challenge, especially for folks who self-drive.

In fact, we need to assure our clients of parking space, before they are willing to visit us in our office. Since we were the first ones to move in, we got the best parking slots and the best prices.

The atmosphere here in the complex is electric and the energy is palpable. You see men and women, all smartly dressed, as they enter the offices with the eagerness to accomplish something meaningful.

On entering the building, you notice the walkways, which are made of glistening granite, where a stream of cleaners makes sure they stay that way. I walked towards the elevator with the same purpose as my fellow comrades. I reached the office, sharp at 9 AM and after the usual biometrics, I was welcomed by a lyrical voice, which I am used to.

"Happy to see you back, Rashi, you look nice!"

"Thanks Amrita, you look thinner today....looks like the new diet is working."

"Thank you so much" she giggled, giving me a beaming smile.

"By the way, how are my appointments lined up today?"

"The client is arriving at 11 AM, the presentation will be followed by a discussion and then you will be proceeding to a business lunch, I have already made the reservations. Before that, you have a catch up with Vikas. He has asked me to let him know the minute you arrive."

"Okay, need a cup of coffee first. Can you get me the usual? An espresso, no sugar"

"Right away, dear!"

Now that I was in my domain, I felt in control.

As I reached my cabin, I saw a lot of post-it notes, pasted on my door. I collected them and started to read some; *Hi Rashi, I hope you get your life back on track, Hi Rashi, congrats on your new assignment; by the way may God help you find a maid. Hi Rashi, please call at this number, maybe you will get some help.....*etc…etc…. They seemed like "*Get Well Soon*" notes, and why not, I had just recovered from the biggest ailment, maidless-ness! I was simply overwhelmed.

As soon as I finished reading the notes extending the awesome emotional support to my ordeal, I realized that I would need to send a thank you note to everyone. I was welcomed by a bouquet of flowers by my immediate team members. They informed me that they had planned to celebrate my promotion through a special snack party in the evening. I was all charged up and ready to take on the day, starting with the catch up with Vikas.

"Hi Vikas"

"Oh hi Rashi, please come in, I wanted to discuss about today's meeting. I must say, your preparation and your inputs have been vital. I think we are well prepared. I just wanted to see you in person, to make sure we are on the same page."

"Makes sense! Is there anything specific that you would like to add or highlight? We have time for me to incorporate any suggestions you may have."

"Not really, but let us go over it together and see if anything needs adjustments. Shall we?"

After the meeting with Vikas, we were fully prepared to tackle the challenge. Our client, popularly known as Muthu, was an elderly gentleman who is a legend in his field. He spoke very little, but when he did, his remarks or suggestions were without fail incredible.

After the presentation, we stood with bated breath, as the period of golden silence sunk in and then he spoke.

"Great pitch Rashi, but the devil lies in the details...hope you will be able to deliver on the commitments made."

"Certainly Muthu, do not worry, we have done this in the past. I personally respect your recommendation and this business is extremely important to our company. Our new brand launch depends on it."

"Consider this done. Rashi, I believe you and hence would trust you with it."

"Thanks Muthu, you won't regret, that's my personal promise."

"Okay great!"

"Let's proceed for lunch; I have made the reservations for your favorite cuisine."

"Oh that's nice, I was not very hungry, but now that you mention it, I am looking forward to the meal. Let's go!"

We walked down to the restaurant, to both build up the appetite, and also to have an extremely productive conversation. During the lunch, we discussed the project and exchanged some suggestions. During my dessert, the gentleman dropped a bomb.

"Rashi, are you free for dinner today? I could introduce you to our group strategy director who, incidentally, is in town. You can talk him through the ideas we discussed today and if time permits, we could deliberate a bit more around the details."

Vikas looked at me apprehensively. I politely declined the request, citing *"husband overseas, temporarily single parent"* as perfectly logical reason. He seemed to accept the decline and didn't appear to be offended.

Once we were back in our office, a deeply satisfied Vikas, after a few deep breaths of possibly relief, commented;

"Rashi, we really nailed it. This can bring us some brilliant business."

"I agree Vikas."

"By the way, Rashi, what really happened with you and your maid?" I narrated the entire episode and he was surprisingly very sympathetic.

"Rashi, do you know that I was the acting housemaid for the entire weekend last week? I cleaned the dishes, dusted the house and trimmed my garden, watered the plants while my wife completed the other tasks. My wife and I were without our regular maid as she had a wedding to attend, which she happened to inform us at the last minute, that too when we called her up!!"

"No matter how much power you have or how much you earn, it ceases to matter once you are back home. The grind gets you at some point, but your episode is especially gruesome. Anyway, wanted to let you know, Sanjay has put in his papers!"

"Oh! When did this happen and why?"

"Yesterday, same reason like everyone – better opportunity." We laughed, when he suddenly enquired, *"Do you know someone who we can hire quickly?"*

"Yes, I know of a fellow from my previous workplace, I will call him up to check if he is interested. Else, I will contact this person I had met at the conference I attended last month. He too will fit the role. Let me work on this."

"Great, that's wonderful! Okay, see you in the evening; I see that your team has prepared a welcome party for you."

At the party, a short 15 minute break, my team had ordered some snacks.

"Welcome back Rashi, we were quite worried for you and wanted to call but this dragon lady here (pointing to Amrita) would not allow us. Meanwhile, we really discussed her idea around the temporary maid service, and maybe someone would launch a service like that someday."

"Yeah, I hope so too...Okay, guys, we have managed a big contract, so congratulations and thanks. I will require all your support and am counting on you to deliver. See you...."

One of my team members followed me; and stopped just outside my cabin.

"Yes, Sumant?"

"Rashi, I need to take around a week's leave, starting 7th of next month. I wanted to speak to you before I applied formally, hope this is Okay."

"What happened?"

"Actually, there is a wedding in the family and we were all planning to go out of town."

"Looks okay, Sumant, please prepare a list of urgent things that are likely to come up during your absence, I hope you will be available on phone. Please tell Riya, to take care of your work in your absence. Consider this approved."

"Thanks, Rashi."

Why can't we have the same professionalism with home staff? I have never declined a leave request from my staff. Everyone in office understands their responsibilities and creates backups before starting their leave. If only….

5:30 PM: I finished off all the important pending tasks. There were still around 100 unread emails, waiting for my attention. What a day! Sun was losing its intensity and twilight was setting in. I managed my final cup of coffee, before redirecting my landline to my cell phone. I was simply tired; I think more from the anxiety of the previous couple of days than by anything else! Auspiciously, on my way out I was welcomed by a cool breeze that had started to flow.

As I walked towards my car, I saw a sea of people on their way out, each of them having a similar look on their faces. I saw a familiar face walk by; *do we have something in common*? Before I could manage to say something, my voice got drowned, partly in the sea of people and partly by the stress of the day. I could also see a few younger groups, planning for their evenings together, maybe at a pub or a restaurant. I was in the same boat, not so long ago!

I revved up my car, switched on the air-conditioning and tuned on to some nostalgic music, let it sink in and then proceeded towards home, fighting the daily traffic. That day, I was extremely tired and too exhausted to take on another battle.

"Mummy how was the day?"

"It was fine, kids. How was yours?"

"Okay" and then after this small chat they went back to watch TV.

"Okay, Madam, may I will leave now?"

"Sure Shanti, see you tomorrow, you will come right?"

"Yes, Madam."

By the time, Sameer arrived on Friday night, I was sound asleep, but I woke up and was I glad to see him…well had it been Mamta, my joy would have been 10 times, but still….. I was relieved, so hugged him tight. The ordeal of the previous week had been an exhausting one. In the morning, when I woke up, I saw the look of bewilderment on his face; as if to say what was all that fuss about! But knowing well what the repercussions of such a question could be, he kept his mouth shut.

Saturday lunch, albeit a pot one, got going at our place. Having rid myself from the title of being maid-less, I was just too exhilarated to let the continuous squabbling of various age groups of kids and the non-stop gossiping of some of the butterflies in our group bother me. But given that our current support were both part-timers and had left well before all the guests said goodbye, house was in a complete mess and there was no way we could just put up our feet and relax.

So Sameer and I got going, trying to bring a semblance of order in the tornado hit house. By the end of it, we were left dead, with our own children looking like vultures roaming about, till I gave in to the urge and bit their head off! Finally, sheer exhaustion took over, and I slept like a log!! The next day, I booked an appointment at the spa for relaxation and rejuvenation as my salvation, after a week of excessive adrenaline rushes.

Rain Rain, Go Away……

After a few months of normalcy ….

I woke up with the alarm at 7 AM; Shanti had still not arrived, Oh God where is she? I frantically tried to call her, but as usual couldn't contact her. It was a Wednesday morning and I had an important meeting. Damn!

This is the biggest challenge with part-timers, everything is fine when they come, but when they don't……And one has no clue as to which day they may decide to go frolicking around!! The feeling of helplessness, which I always feel at this last minute no-show, is simply overwhelming. But then I recollected, I had no time to brood, so pulled up my socks and those of Sameer's as well….

"Sameer, wake up!"

Sameer opened his groggy eyes...

"Shanti is probably not coming today"

"What?"

"Wake up quickly, Shanti is not coming! You know the back-up routine.....Wake up the kids and get them ready, and I will rush to the kitchen..."

"Rashi, you know I had a late night with colleagues and am still very tired. Can't the kids skip it today? Why can't I sleep in peace for today?"

"Okay, then who is going to manage the kids today, if they stay at home?" I asked pointedly.

"I can't, as I have meetings...Oh!" Sameer got up with a start as the gravity of the situation dawned upon him.

Meanwhile, I was frantically trying to reach Shanti alternately dialing her two phones, one smart and one dumb (I still wonder which one is the smarter one) which she has, I even send her a text message and a WhatsApp message without luck. Well, I could try messaging her on Facebook, I thought.

I checked my calendar to see if I had any important appointments in the afternoon. Maybe I could pick the kids up in the afternoon. Oh no! One of our clients was visiting us today afternoon and his visit could get extended to evening as well. I checked with Sameer, if he could come back early. He declined as he had some very critical meeting in the evening and he expected to be back at his usual time. So I had to send them to a playschool nearby who picks them up directly from school.

This was the playschool they had gone to years ago, and as it also had a day school, I had used their facility a number of times before the era of full time maid descended on me. This is the super emergency back-up plan, which comes in handy at least a couple of times a month, when something like this happens.

This reminded me to put up a suggestion in the office for a need to have tie-up with a crèche and a van to ferry the kids from the school for emergencies like today, which are not unique to me. But at that time, with no such facility, I needed to manage on my own. Meanwhile, the chaos continued! Getting kids and their father ready has always been a tough ask, having accomplished that, I asked Sameer to drop the kids to the bus stop.

"Papa we are getting late, we will miss the bus today."

"Just give me two more minutes."

"Sameer, if they miss the bus, please plan to drop them at the school."

"Rashi PLEASE, can't a guy have two seconds of peace in the loo!"

"Forget it, I am taking them to the stop, you read your useless paper."

Poor old me, as always, gets the rough end of the stick. After all, for everyone I am the backup plan. Sameer knows pretty well that I hate it when kids miss their bus, so he takes advantage of this. Anyway, on my way, I called up the playschool and with the emergency protocol process locked in, I returned from the bus stop, tired and vanquished.

Every time I use this backup plan, I have this strange apprehension. *What if something goes wrong? What if they forget to pick up the kids? What if my kids get ill after the stress of being away from home the whole day?* I shook off this feeling thinking this had always worked in the past, hence there was no reason it shouldn't work that time. I pay the minimum retainer charges at the playschool every month, for such days. This is like the insurance plan you buy, with the hope that you never need to use.

I changed, and as I was about to leave for office, I got a message on WhatsApp, "*Madam, it's raining heavily today, all lanes are blocked, I cannot come out of my house*"

Stunned but helpless, there was nothing I could do .....I cursed the rain, my circumstances and my situation but what cannot be cured has to be endured!

I replied politely *"No issues Shanti, I can understand. You enjoy the day with tea and pakoras......"*

As I walked towards my car with the umbrella in my hand (yes, it was raining heavily), I could understand the girl's plight, but who would understand mine!

Poor Shanti, having to bear the brunt of the rain gods in her tiny little hutment, I felt pity for her. With her lanes blocked and water flooding her house, it would be some work for her to get the water out of her house and getting it up and running. I felt guilty that I was only worrying about myself without understanding the plight of the less privileged. As repentance, I thought I would compensate some of the damage that the rain may have caused in her house. After all, it was her dedicated services because of which my household was running smoothly. The least I could do for her was to help her when there was a crisis in her life!

I navigated the roads with great difficulty. It's a shame that how, with a just a couple of hours of rain, all the good roads on the city become completely jammed, with water clogged on the sides and two wheeler riders crowding under the bridges to escape the rain. All this ensures that less than a third of the road is available for commuting. As for the poor car commuters, in case the wipers are not working or if a pothole exists under the puddle of water and one is unaware, it can be their doomsday.

Despite the obstacles, I managed to reach office on time. Back in my office den, I immersed myself in loads of work, as I put my team to prepare the draft for the event, which I had promised to the client. Suddenly the reminder for the meeting of Women's Network event in the conference room popped up on my screen.

I put up the suggestion for a crèche and a van in the forum, but since it was expected to be utilized only in emergency situations and was to be a paid facility, there were hardly any takers for the proposition. My co-workers were concerned about the security aspects of the same as well. So basically the idea was a non-starter!! I wondered why. Maybe I was too thick into the situation and hence thought this was a real need, maybe they all had strong backup plans; family or friends who could chip in…..

Anyway, this was worth a try, it might succeed later when more people start to feel the pinch. I grabbed my coffee and went back to work, kept checking on the kids regularly with the play school. Things seemed to be moving smoothly so far.

As I watched the people below in the evening, I started to think….*why me? Is this only me or are there others around who share the same pain and the helplessness that I feel.*

I was about to leave when there was a knock on my door. Vedika, a colleague, entered my cabin. I was hard pressed for time but Vedika was a single mother, estranged, on her way to a divorce. She had a son at home and there was no support forthcoming from her estranged husband as court proceedings were pending. Besides, she had ailing old parents. Her father was running a small local shop in their hometown. They barely managed their lives and could hardly support her in these trying times. I knew she had a maid, whom she had got from her native place, who used to hold her house together while Vedika was at work. Given her situation, I always took care that I addressed her issues promptly, whenever possible.

"Hi Rashi, hope I am not disturbing."

"No... not at all, do come in."

"Rashi, I am having problems around my domestic help and don't know who to discuss this with. Since I saw you quite vocal in the Women's network with suggestions, hence I thought maybe you can possibly help."

You have come to the wrong person I thought, but smiled and said, *"Sure Vedika, what's up?"*

"Rashi, I have a situation at home, my maid as you know, is from my hometown and she is ill. She is my backbone and it seems my backbone has stretched to the limit. She started coughing over the past month and we had not given it much thought. On seeing that the cough is not going away, I took her to the doctor to get a checkup. The doctor has diagnosed her with Tuberculosis. Now, this is truly worrisome!! I am worried for her and will ensure she gets best treatment. But I am also worried about Vihaan; he has been exposed to her all the time. She is more of a mom to him and he is glued to her all the time. Now, with this situation, I am at my wits end, as to what to do. I thought maybe you can help me think through this."

I was taken aback and then reached out to the recesses of my mind to think of the possible options.

After this moment of catharsis, Vedika started crying, so I asked her to sit down. "*Amrita, get some tea for Vedika, please.*"

As she sipped hot tea, I pacified her a little,

"Vedika, please stop worrying. You have a number of options. You know that TB is curable, you just need to follow the medicines and the routine, so you can ask your maid to get on to the medicines as soon as possible."

"Option one is to get her treatment done here in the city, where you have access to the best doctors and the treatment. You would need to create some space for her in your house, a little away from Vihaan. You can discuss with the doctor on the precautions that need to be taken. For your house work, you need to hire some help temporarily who can work so that your own maid can relax and her recovery is faster. Once she recovers, she can come back to her old routine and you can go back to yours."

"Alternately, you can send your maid to her hometown, where she can relax and stay with her parents and get the treatment. Again, you will need to hire temporary help till the time this gets over. I would suggest that you discuss the options with her and jointly decide what to do next."

"One thing I can assure you though, I will make sure that from office front you are not loaded, and we can also work out one or two days of working from home for a few weeks."

"Thanks Rashi, I am overwhelmed by your suggestions and your support and I feel more relaxed now. I will keep you posted. Okay, thanks once again and bye." She seemed little less burdened than a few minutes ago.

It is so strange that when you are immersed in your own problems, you seem to miss out on thinking objectively, possibly because your emotions are interfering with your mind. However, when it is used for others, you seem to come up with best solutions.

After this discussion, I was completely drained, both physically and mentally.

As I was driving back, I looked out and saw many other women carrying the same forlorn look. I was tempted to ask them what was on top of their minds right then and I thought I had a good sense what they would say.........

I was brought back to my senses by a blaring horn, someone was shouting, saying, "*Move, lady, you are blocking the traffic, lady drivers...*"

*U*gh! I seemed to have made a habit of daydreaming!! I drove off promptly to pick up the kids and hopefully some pakoras, bhajiya and vadapav on the way....Cheers....

After picking up the kids from the playschool and settling them in the house, just as I was planning to relax a bit, Sajida came in. (I had requested her to come late today). As Sajida and I sat down to have our tea together, she enquired.

"Madam, did Shanti turn up today?"

"No, all her lanes were blocked and she was stuck in her house."

"Stuck in her house, you say? Madam, it is strange, first of all, her hutment is on the hill, and she has a road leading away from the ditch so water cannot collect there. Moreover, I saw her on a motorcycle with some guy, all dressed up. I was wondering, if you had given her a holiday" silently sliding in the message that she might need an off later. And planting doubts about her honesty in my mind! "*Oh, maybe, she wanted to have a good time today."*

Saying this she left after completing her work, leaving me to clean up and FUME!

"Honey, I'm home.....Need me to clean up something?"

Aftermath, Politics of Two Maids

From that day onwards, I started to notice the buildup of quiet hostility between the two maids. They seemed to be at each other's space, felt as if they were having a mental wrestling match.

Sajida did not stop at just giving me the information. She probably asked Shanti if she had lied to me and, more annoyingly, wanted to know the details of the motorcycle ride. I believe Shanti had snubbed Sajida and that had put them in the cross paths. This left me struggling to keep up with the cold war.

To confirm the validity of Sajida's story, I spoke with Shanti directly the next day. She promptly replied that once the weather had given way, she had gone on a long drive with her boyfriend.....

Boyfriend? Now that was a new variable....

"I hope you do not invite him to our house in my absence."

"No Madam, he is a decent fellow, works as a driver in the next lane, you can check his references. Besides, it's nothing serious, we exchanged a couple of messages on the phone and he asked me out yesterday for a drive, it was fun."

Indeed it was fun day, even for me! I thought, rolling my eyes over.

"Okay and what about the water-logging?"

"Oh madam, you don't need to worry, the house is on a raised area, after some time, the water just recedes."

"Really? Your message sounded desperate"...I said sarcastically...

"Actually madam, I was scared but then things changed so quickly, what to do...anyway I have come today, haven't I?" She had a point!

I started to say something but then shut up. I thought that this was her personal affair and I should not go around offering any unwarranted advice. Minding my own business seemed to be the best strategy at that time, but I couldn't shake off a feeling of impeding danger!

Soon, the blame game between Sajida and Shanti started.

"Shanti, there is water on the floor of the kitchen, why is it not cleaned up? Someone could slip in this mess and break a leg."

"Madam, it is Sajida's job to clean up after her work, she misses it regularly. I wanted to tell you this, now you can see for yourself."

"Sajida, please can you clean the overspill of water in the kitchen after you are done!" I told Sajida the next day.

"Madam, I do it, but then the water trickles down anyway. Maybe there is a leak in the basin, can you get that checked? Also Shanti has to clean the house so she can do it in case of these spillovers."

"Madam, Sajida regularly drinks tea when she comes to cook the food."

"Shanti, I have told her to have tea, if she wants, as she has to complete a lot of chores and walk a lot. I do not see a big issue in this."

"Madam, having tea is okay, but she leaves her tea cup and the plate for others to clean up. That is not right, is it? One should be responsible for ones work."

"Yes, indeed."

This was snowballing into a big issue; allegations and counter allegations. It was beginning to look like our news channels these days, where no one lets another speak, and everyone fights over any and every thing!!

And what role does Rashi Jindal, VP of a large conglomerate, have in all this; Managing Egos! I think this is part of the process here; I need some skills to manage these power-plays and some mentoring. I wondered what more was in store.....

Golf Expendition

*"**M**ehak, Muskan, remember we have to go for golf lessons today.....Wake up."*

"Come on, Sameer, its Sunday...let us be..." I pulled under the blanket, hoping this could go away *"Switch off the light, Sameer."*

"Papa, let us sleep..." and then they also rolled inside the blanket.

"Kids, remember we had made this program, last month, I have already fixed up with the pro and don't want to be late. You will get pro lessons. Sandy uncle and his family are coming over, they will reach the club and we don't want to be late, do we?"

"Guys, I have got my new set of irons which I want to break into. All of you have your own set of clubs, which have been gathering dust for quite some time, let us get some exercise and fun. Come on, don't be lazy, get up and get going."

I wished Sameer stopped these insistent ramblings! I am not a sportsperson and I always fear that I might pull a muscle or two, by just holding the iron with the proper grip. Ah! But the food at the club is awesome and I don't mind the splurge on desserts. With this I drifted into my dreams filled with dessert, mousses, pastries, tiramisu, soufflés, pies, wow!

"Wakey, Wakey...." Sameer started to make noises again.

"Rashi, get up, dear. This is not done, whenever I make a program, there is always some excuse."

"Hope Shanti is here...."

"Rashi, please hurry up..."

"I hate these golf sessions.... I have to get all dressed up to concentrate on hitting a small ball, which by some way or the other always evades me. I would be lucky if I could manage a few touches."

I have told this to Sameer a number of times but he refuses to listen. His obsession runs amok and gets painful when you look at the expenses and the space requirements. Sometimes, I think about disposing everything off, but the fear of his wrath, that I will then incur, prevents me from attempting to do so. Maybe someday I will pick up the courage to give these away, on the sly. My garage is full of things that need to be given away; broken stuff, discarded stuff, stuff that is now forgotten.

Although I must admit the golf greens did have the 'right' atmosphere. Here you would meet the top corporate professionals and their spouses, casually but smartly dressed, as you try to make the right impression, sit and chat with them over the relaxed atmosphere of the club and the game; but of course the most enticing of all; THE FOOD.

"Mummy, I can't find my lucky T-shirt..."

"Didi, please locate my hair band...."

"Shanti, I can't seem to find my golf shoes. Where have you kept them?"

"Can you also locate my golf balls, while you are searching for the shoes?"

"Let me call the club to check if they have confirmed our reservations for the lunch."

"Let me take out my new set of irons that I have bought. Yes, here they are, what a beauty, aren't, they? I will unwrap them at the club, let Sandy also take a look."

"Mehak, please clean up your and Muskan's clubs. We do not want to look dirty, do we? And please keep some band-aid with you. Last time while playing, you had a sore thumb. This time, let us be more prepared. Also pack an umbrella, in case it rains."

After the whirlwind of morning chores, we were finally ready to leave.

Time for some instructions to Shanti.

"Shanti, we are going out for the day, will be back by late noon. Meanwhile, please clean up the house, wash the utensils. Please keep the house locked so that no one comes over, understood. We should be back after lunch."

"Okay, madam."

I had an uneasy feeling that she was watching my back, but I shook it off.

We reached the club and were greeted by the regulars. Sameer was behaving like a kid and the pro had already reached the driving range. We walked down to the driving range and requested for some practice balls.

Next came the part that I hate, which are the golf lessons themselves. We met the pro at the driving range, who was all geared up for the challenge.

"Madam, please line up your feet and the grip, shoulders in line, stomach in, and take a practice shot." Swoosh! No contact, okay no problem.

The pro had tried hard to teach me the skills, what with the grip, the shoulders and the toes but the hardest part for me comes, when I have to put it all together to connect the club with the ball. With all the might, the best I managed was a sputter of a shot at the end.

"Golf is a game of patience and concentration madam, please practice more. Now I will move to Sameer Sir," he quickly scooted, leaving me to deal with the balls and my fate. Meanwhile, kids were enjoying themselves, especially Muskan, who by now, had started to make contact with the ball. Mehak was on the end of the range, practicing her putting with a few other girls.

My daughters seemed to hit better than I could ever imagine, and after a few shots, I was content to sit out the rest of the show with an energy drink and a snack in tow, along with Mehak, who had finished her putting practice.

Then Sandy and his wife arrived, with their maid in tow, fully geared up to meet Sameer's challenge. Sandy and his wife Trish have been our friends for some time. The common love of golf between the two husbands and the common crisis, called maids, between the two wives had brought us closer over the years. With Trish, I had a variety of common topics to discuss, hence we could keep ourselves occupied and engaged. But as always, somehow the conversation always got steered towards our favorite topic of domestic help and their idiosyncrasies.

Trish is not working now, though she used to earlier and managed the household pretty well, her schedules are all worked out and she keeps her back up plans ready. Even though we call her a war veteran, she also loses the battles and becomes as helpless as any other woman, when it comes to managing the idiosyncrasies of house support staff

Trish started telling me some of her interesting stories and she was careful to start this conversation only when her maid and our children were out of sight.

Apparently, Trish had developed this new fetish about 'Impact of technology on maid society!' *"Rashi, don't let them out alone. They come back with loads of phone numbers and even handsets gifted to them by strangers. This is like feeding the worm to catch the fish. Ever since these cell phones have been invented and become so affordable; it has become the bane of all our problems."*

Next came her ever entertaining anecdotes! She did seem to have a repertoire of stories on this topic. An aunt of hers had arrived from the US; she had got some of her old clothes which she wanted to give away. They were in very good condition, and from top US brands. When she offered this to Trish's maid, she politely refused and hinted she'd prefer money as a reward.

Next day, she was wearing a swanky top, which was an exact copy of a branded item. Anxious, the aunt asked the maid to take her to place where the latter shops. And lo and behold, they were gone for the whole day, bringing back quite a few 'branded' clothes. Now even after her aunt is gone, she exchanges notes with this girl on WhatsApp on the latest trends and prices in these shops in India.

Another interesting tale was from another continent! Trish's sister in law, Amla, was visiting from Canada, and when Trish started discussing about how challenging managing household work with its series of providers is, she unwittingly had touched a raw nerve. It seems that Canada also has its share of domestic help with most of them coming from Asian countries like the Philippines. They seem to work on an hourly basis with fixed timings. One day when Amla's regular help in Canada went back to her home country, she started inquiring around as to whether she can get some help for the time being.

What happened next was pretty funny, I would say. She had this close friend of hers who had a very efficient maid. When Amla asked her, on their WhatsApp group, for her contact details, three other ladies immediately interjected, forbidding her friend from sharing any details. She realized that her friend and these three ladies were taking the services of the same maid. Her time was divided between the four of them and they feared that if a fifth assignment came her way, she would not perform her duties properly at their place.

Sameer had meanwhile lined up his new expensive set of irons showing off amongst his friends, while managing only a few good shots. It was amusing that how with his extremely limited skills he was boasting about like a champ! It was a bit embarrassing too but then I know all wives have to undergo this mortification because men do tend to become kids in front of their friends and parents.

Anyway, we were really enjoying, when the weather took an unexpected turn. The sky became dark and looked like we were in for a very heavy rain. We rushed to the clubhouse and then prepared for the drive back home.

"Rashi, what a mess! We would need to go back home as we are early for lunch at the club. I will go and cancel the reservations and get the car. Meanwhile please round up the kids, we are going home."

While on our way back, I had to listen to the exaggerated display of emotions from Sameer who was really disappointed.

"Damn, it was not meant to be my day. Just when I was perfecting my drive and was about to beat Sandy, the rain Gods took away the prospect, by appearing at the wrong time. That bugger Sandy got away this time. He always beats me in the game and today when I had more than a fair chance to beat him, this happened. Didn't you see my skills today? What do you think?"

Before I could muster my thoughts to conjure something up, thankfully, Sameer continued with his discourse and I continued my luxury of being switched off mentally.

"Oh you should have seen the swing with my new driver, awesome, one of the balls just went out of the park."

"Oh really, did it go sideways....." I muttered, but there was no stopping Sameer. I had my own worries; I had not

planned for lunch at home, so I thought I had better call up Shanti to start preparation for lunch. Then I thought kids would be disappointed, so maybe we could order some food to be delivered at our place.

"Kids, are you okay to have pizza?" I asked a rhetorical question….and got an excited affirmative. I immediately ordered pizza using an app so that by the time we were to reach home the pizza would be delivered. The kids wanted to have some coke and Sameer wanted to pick up beer, so they dropped me home before going to the nearby store.

When I reached the house, I sensed something was amiss. I could not put a finger to it, but I could sense that something was not right. I managed to reach the main door and instead of ringing the bell, I opened it with my master key.

The house was uncannily dark, very unlike our house. I keep all the curtains open so as to get natural light. I don't know why, but I was tip-toeing in my own house as if I was a thief and I felt uncomfortable. I realized that the house was in complete mess; Shanti had not bothered to clean up. The half-eaten plates were still on the table and the covers on the sofa were strewn around the place. The clothes were still there in the basket waiting to be soaked for washing. I wondered what Shanti was doing.

I thought to shout for Shanti but strangely the words did not come out.

I went in and there was darkness in the hallway. I saw a small light coming through my bedroom door, which was ajar. When, I opened the door, I was aghast at the sight……… the neighborhood driver and Shanti were in my bed, naked…..enjoying themselves, with our favorite bottle of wine, I was so sick….

"Get out!"

"Madam, I can explain, he is my fiancé."

"Get out, I say…..this very minute, I told you, never invite your boyfriend in my house, you can have sex wherever you want but not in my house and most definitely not in my bed….." I was fuming and extremely disgusted.

They picked up their clothes and left through the back door and I was glad that Sameer and the kids were not there to watch this event. It was left for me to clean up the mess.

Apparently, the moment Shanti learnt that we were all going out; she had called up her paramour and asked him to come over. I recalled Trish's words *"maids with mobile phones are a pain!"*

"I told you so, Madam", Sajida exclaimed. *"I was not comfortable with her attitude from the day she lied about the water-logging. God knows, how many times they have done it earlier."* I was in no mood to listen to her banter.

Sameer was quite furious about the encounter, though I think he was more concerned about his favorite wine being consumed, than the fact that they were using our bedroom.

By now the entire neighborhood had come to know about the escapades, as it had spread like wild fire. The neighbors kept giving us penetrating looks as if we were involved in some unholy alliances!! I had never felt so hurt, humiliated and violated in my life. *What have I done to deserve this?*

I felt disgusted and felt the need to hibernate till this was forgotten.

I was soon granted my wish when an aggressive catfight over parking, which got nasty subsequently, replaced the maid story for juicy gossip. Public memory is too short and too forgiving.

With Sajida's help, I trudged along in my life, as slowly the story faded into oblivion.

Sisters – Shared Karma

Interestingly my sister, Preeti, in Pune seemed to be sharing the maid karma with me. Similar set of continuous churn of unpredictable, unreliable, unethical and arrogant maids seemed to be her story as well. After the usual preliminaries, she started sharing her troubles with me.

"My in laws are expected to be with us from next week and I am struggling to find a new maid and a cook."

"What happened?"

This girl whom she had hired just three months ago turned out to be a weird character.

"The other day, I saw her putting her hand inside some street dog's mouth stating she was just feeding it and it would not bite. As if this was not enough, one day she was dipping her face inside the bucket of water she was mopping the floor with! When I asked her, why she was doing this, she said it was very hot and water inside the bucket was acting like a cooler for her."

"About a month ago, she started acting grumpy all the time. I asked her repeatedly for the cause of her unhappiness. She accused our cook of forcing himself on her when we were all away for a family function!! I was stunned!!

My first thought was that I should report this to the police and get the cook punished and hence I started asking some details so that the report could be made. I asked her to narrate, when and how the cook entered the house. As you know, we had given her a servant room on the top floor of our house. She said she opened the door and took him upstairs as he was pestering her. After a bit of probing, it became clear that she had informed him about our absence and had willingly taken him to her room and when things started getting too hot for her to handle, she pushed him out of the room.

You can imagine Rashi, by that time we were all feeling a bit concerned. We had realized that though there had been no forced sexual contact, we needed to be careful. The girl herself was not too reliable. So the next few days I started keeping her away from the kitchen when our cook was here and kept an eagle's eye on her movements.

"Last week, I had gone for a very critical meeting and Rajan was to come home early. When he came home, he was shocked. This girl was hanging around the cook's neck and Rajan caught them in the act from our kitchen window!! And mind you, this cook is married with kids. I fired both of them on the spot."

"Frankly, I am scared of keeping anyone new but don't know how long I can manage the entire household by myself. What about you? Have you had any luck?"

So I shared my plight with her.

"Oh my God, you know about a year and a half back I had a very similar trauma."

And then she narrated her equally harrowing experience….

Preeti's Woes

(The following is a narrative by Preeti and hence the "I" here is for Preeti)

Vimla was the best maid I had had, ever since I got married, and started taking responsibility of managing a household

I still remember it was 20 February last year; the morning had begun as beautifully as ever, with a delicious cup of tea and some hilarious messages. Ananya did resist going to school on that day, as previous evening we had attended a friend's wedding, but somehow 'Vimla Didi' had cajoled her to get up and get ready.

"She does have a way with the kids. She always manages them to get ready for school even if they are reluctant," I mentioned to Rajan.

"You are right! She loves the home alone time too much to let anyone stay at home when it's not a holiday. One of these days we should come home unannounced to see what she is up to," laughed Rajan.

Little did either of us know how prophetic this statement would turn out to be!!

With kids gone to school, Rajan and I left the house at our usual time even though both of us were feeling a bit tired. Thanks to none other than the super-efficient Vimla, who took care of even the tiniest tasks we normally do ourselves, we were able to take up the challenge of going to office that day.

"Preeti, we have done it again, the contract is ours!!" Anand, my boss, came beaming*; "What would we do without you!!"*

And just then the phone rang, *"Am I speaking to Ananya Gupta's mother." "Yes",* I replied anxiously. *"Well ma'am she has been sick since she came to school and has slight fever as well. We would advice that you take her home."*

After informing Anand, I rushed to the school to pick up my baby; feeling an insurmountable burden of guilt!! *Why could I not allow her to take off, I knew she had not got enough sleep!! But no, I have to get to office as I have this meeting that can't be done without the indispensable me..... What kind of a mother am I!*

Just now Anand mentioned what they would have done without me; and I, in my own self-importance, have been taking that literally. Office existed before me and would continue after me, but my kids..... How could I be so un-motherly, lacking in compassion when it came to my own baby.

The moment I reached school, Ananya came and hugged me. She was sobbing, *"Mummy, my head is hurting, Ma'am gave me some medicine to stop my vomits, but my head...Boohoo ho!"*

I engulfed her in my arms, checked about the medicines given so far and went to her doctor's.

"Don't worry Ms. Preeti, it's just a bit of exertion and a mild infection, am giving her a mild antibiotic, an anti-histamine and something for her fever, give her these and some rest, she should be fine soon. Don't send her to school

for next two days." On my way to home, I called up Anand and told him I had to take a couple of days off.

On reaching home, just when I was about to ring the bell, it struck me that this is early noon and maybe Vimla would be taking a short nap. So instead of ringing the bell, I used my keys to open the door and took Ananya to my room.........

As I reached closer to my room, I saw that the dim light in my room was on and some soft music was playing! I was a bit perplexed, but didn't think much of it, till I opened the door and stood shocked!!!

There was my incredible maid, making out with some creep in MY BED!! I immediately blocked the sight from Ananya, took her to her room, wrapped her in her blanket and went BACK. By now, both of them had got dressed and Vimla was cowering in fear. I looked menacingly at them and told both of them to get the hell out of my house in five minutes flat, beyond which I would report them to the police on charges of trespassing. Vimla collected her bag and the two of them went out in a jiffy. I tore out the entire bedding and threw it out in the verandah!! Swallowing my disgust and despair, I moved back to Ananya who needed my immediate attention.

A few hours later, after playing the perfect caring mother of a sick child and getting her to sleep, I went to the verandah. The bedcovers lying there were a gift by mummy on my 10th wedding anniversary; an intense blue that had dark impressions looking like a raging sea. It was one of my favorite beddings, and I had used it very occasionally. Just a month back, on Rajan's insistence, I had started using it regularly. And it is on this bedding....... the hideous image of that maid and her paramour flashed through my mind and all I could see was blue fire!! I immediately called up the agent.

"What happened Madam, hope Vimla is doing fine?"

"Fine, she is doing more than fine, she has been on her honeymoon on a private suite with all meals paid."

"What happened Madam, you sound really upset!"

After I narrated the gory details of what had been happening in my heavenly abode, I asked him for replacement

"I have one, not as good as Vimla but reliable. She is semi trained, so you will have to manage cooking veggies on your own. She can make chapattis, tea, coffee etc."

"OK, when can you bring her?"

"Today itself if you want, but I would draw a new contract for her."

"What does that mean?"

"I will draw a 12 month contract, the commission remains the same, so I would adjust 9 months commission against the previous contract, and you pay the three months commission."

Sure, I agreed, more than happy that the next hunt would start after a year instead of nine months. So, in the next hour, our new maid Muniya was introduced, interviewed and put on the job.

Duh!

I was relaxed as I was on leave for the next few days and so could train Muniya. However, I was also clear on my priorities. I had taken these days off for my child and no turmoil in the other fronts of life could deter me, thanks to the major guilt trip I had recently been on!

"But first things first; what do we do for dinner? Ordering something is out of question, Ananya's present condition ruled that out. Aha, the good old khichdi (risotto for Europeans, a mixture of rice and pulses cooked together with minimal spices) would be good on everyone's stomach." Of course the fact that it's one of the least effort food item added to its attractiveness.

Just as I started giving instructions to Muniya on getting the ingredients ready, Manu yelled with a long suffering voice; *"Hope, you are not planning to make khichdi tonight, you have this pathetic habit of giving us that totally unpalatable dish as soon as the maid changes".*

That comment, on top of my guilt trip, was too much, and just as I pumped air in my lungs to give a big shout of rage, Rajan said softly, *"Darling son, that's so true, given that Mummy is busy with Ananya and YOU would not like to have khichdi, why don't you help peel and cut potatoes so that I can make your favorite dish with it. And we'll have to do that quickly as its past eight and we all are very hungry".*

"Dad, I am watching Big Bang theory till 9."

"Great, if you can't help in the cooking stop complaining. Preeti, please go ahead and make whatever you think is best suited."

"Thanks Rajan," I muttered.

Not sure about how Ananya's health would progress through the night, I clearly explained to Muniya where the ingredients were for our morning tea and what time I would need it.

"Mummy, my head is hurting;" whispered Ananya in the middle of night. Sleepily, I touched her head and jolted out of my bed. *"Rajan, Ananya seems to have very high fever"*, I muttered. No Reaction! As the panic starting building up, I slowly breathed in and out twice, and reached out to the thermometer to check the temperature; 103° F!

"Rajan, please get up. Ananya's fever is skyrocketing, we need to bring it down immediately", I shouted panicking. When I was young, one of my very bright classmates had lost her brilliance due to very high temperature that impacted her brain. Since then, no amount of 'gyaan' from experts that each individual has his or her own threshold and we should not generalize on this, helped my rational thinking process, and my fuse used to go off every time someone in the family had fever beyond 102° F!!

"What time did you give her the medicines, can we give her another dose of Paracetamol?"

"6 hours back, yes we can administer another dose. You give the med; I will get cold water and cloth for cold compression."

It took us about 40-45 minutes to get her temperature under control. We managed to get to bed by 3 AM, but I couldn't sleep due to the fear that the temperature may again shoot up.

Bang! Bang!

"Who's it?"

"Madam, it's Muniya, you said you need tea at 6. I cannot find the milk."

"Milk is in the Fridge."

"What?"

"It's in the fridge."

"Madam what is that?"

"You don't know what a fridge is!!"

Having a severe headache, my patience was at an all-time low, but there was no point getting worked up first thing in the morning. So I came out to give milk to the so called 'semi trained' maid. I told her firmly to make the tea as soon as possible. Ten minutes later she came in with something that looked very much like brown soapy water!!

"What have you made?"

"Tea!"

"And how did you make it?"

"I put some water, some tea leaves and some milk and boiled it."

"And how much of each did you put?"

"Half glass water, half teaspoon tea leaves and one glass milk."

"Raja.....n!"

"Hey what happened? Why are you looking like you are going to burst apart?" Rajan mumbled waking up with a start.

"Can you please get me a cup of tea, I will die without it and this girl has no clue, whatsoever, of how tea is made. I couldn't sleep the whole night, and now this, I..."

"Ok.... Ok... I am up! You will have your tea in next 2 minutes."

I told Muniya to have her tea, keep the rest aside, and then to cut some potatoes and knead some dough so that I could make Manu's favorite dish. Then finally I got in the bed for a short nap.

After having a nice cup of tea made by my only permanent savior, I quickly woke up Manu, made the breakfast and saw him off to his school.

Ananya was still fast asleep and Rajan's lunch was packed. I felt like having a cup of coffee

"Rajan, would you like to have a cup of coffee?"

"Preeti, I really do not have time to make one, I do have this very important client meeting."

"Hey, I'm not expecting you to do this..."

"Are you going to ask HER to make it, sorry..."

"Oh no, absolutely not, I will make it. Muniya, come, I am making coffee, let me teach you how this extremely critical beverage is made."

As the day went by, I realized Muniya had no experience whatsoever of doing any household chores. She had been engaged as a baby sitter with a young couple and all she had to do was play with the kid and feed her. It dawned on me that in the parlance of the agents in this city, anyone who has spent a year or two as a domestic help, is known as semi trained.

At lunch, I patiently taught her how to make chapattis so that I could get some support in the kitchen. In between the periods that Ananya needed me, I spent the remaining day, explaining the things that I needed Muniya to handle and how it had to be done. At night I went to bed exhausted but with a satisfaction that from tomorrow the things would be easier. Ah! Little did I know!!

Two weeks had passed since Muniya came into our house. I had stopped asking her for tea or chapattis, as I could not bear the ensuing drama.

"Muniya, I had asked you to iron my clothes first. Can you please leave the washing and come here immediately!"

No response

"Can't you hear me you idiot!! I have been telling you since the last two weeks, washing of clothes and cleaning of

house is to be done AFTER we leave for office. Right now you need to work on priority items."

No response

I went into the room, stopped the washing machine, and firmly took her to the iron board.

"Preeti, where is my white shirt? I am not able to find it anywhere in my cupboard," Rajan came out shouting

"Here it is, I found it in Manu's cupboard."

"MUNIYA, YOU CANNOT BE THIS STUPID. How come you cannot distinguish between the shirt of a 12 year old and a 40 year old!!"

This is when I suddenly stopped myself;

Oh God!! What is becoming of me!! I am known as a person who maintains her cool at the most stressful of times, and here I have used words like 'Idiot' and 'Stupid' in a single conversation!! This is not me; respecting dignity of human beings is a non-negotiable value that we have grown up with.

That day I decided, no matter what the level of provocation, I will never use abusive words! I could not let a young 20-year-old change my basic values. I decided that moment that I would start meditation to take away the collective stress of a demanding career, growing kids…. growing into the rebellious teenagers, incompetent domestic helper and what more. Well as they say, there always is a silver lining to every cloud, Muniya and her unbelievable ineptitude initiated me into a lifelong practice of meditation.

Complementary Worker

A week later, as I was leaving for office, Mrs. Malhotra from the next house called out to me asking if I was looking for a cook.

"Oh yes, Aunty! You are a godsend!!"

"I overheard Rajan sharing with your uncle how dumb your maid is and how tough life has become for you. So I decided I should find you some external help. I have not seen anyone work so hard, you are such a darling. I remember when your uncle fell down and you had rushed him to the hospital leaving your critical meeting...."

"Aunty," I interrupted embarrassed, *"you were talking about a cook...."*

"Oh dear, the cook! Well there is this cook, Suman, who works at one of my friends place. Do you know Mrs. Singhal? Suman has been cooking for her for the last two years and she mentioned she is looking for some more work, so I took her number for you. Here take it."

"Thanks a ton Aunty!! I will speak to her at the earliest."

"Do that, Mrs. Singhal, being a great cook herself, is not easy to please. So if this woman has managed to work at her place for two years she has to be good."

Thanking her once again I sat into my car and immediately called Suman. Wow!! ....At least one major task is taken care of!!

Suman turned out to be a great cook indeed. Not only could she make the normal chapatti, vegetables, pulses and rice; she seemed to turn up with delicious noodles, mouth-watering pavbhaji, sumptuous south Indian dishes, awesome pizzas, pastas, and what not. Manu and Ananya were pampered like never before. Every other day they made demands for some new dish; which as a vigilant mother, I had to curtail to once, or at most twice, a week.

A few months of bliss but all good things must come to an end.

Rajan had been on a tour for a week and was supposed to return that evening. I had decided to get his favorite daal-baati-churma made. Suman had proven her expertise in Rajasthani dishes as well.

Just as I reached the door to leave…

*"Didi, salt and sugar are about to finish, please order for more;"*called out Muniya

"Hey, we got a kg of salt just last week and of sugar two weeks back!! How come it's finished so quickly?"

"I don't know, but see it's not there."

Alarmed, I started checking my other groceries as well. *Something is amiss…*I decided to scan through my expense book. *Good lord, my grocery expense has almost doubled in the last three months!! It cannot be simply more usage, there has to be pilferage.*

I called up Mrs. Singhal.

"Hello Aunty, this is Preeti..."

"Oh yes, how are you doing beta? Is your cook problem sorted out? Mrs. Malhotra told me about you and how one after the other you've had a disaster on domestic help front."

"Am fine Aunty, have called up to check something about Suman."

"Yes, what about her, is she troubling you?"

Very hesitatingly I started; "*well aunty, she is a wonderful cook.....it's just that since she has come in, my grocery bill has doubled. So I was wondering....I mean, is it...."*

"Oh, I forgot to mention that to Mrs. Malhotra, Suman is a hardened thief; she does pilferage stuff from your kitchen if you are not careful. It's just that her cooking is so good that I have continued with her. But it is a headache to maintain a watch on her."

"Oh, so you watch over her?"

"Yes, absolutely! I keep an eye in the kitchen as long as she is in there."

"Hmmm... Ok thanks Aunty, I too will have to find a way."

But it wasn't that easy for me as I reached home late and she was gone by then. I took a copy and started listing down my options.

- Confront her...*she will refuse. What proof do I have? If I insist, I run the risk of losing her; ruled out!!*
- Come early from office....*Not feasible everyday*
- Ask her to come late......*why would she agree?*
- Keep very limited quantity in her reach....*again not feasible in the long run*
- Ask Manu to keep an eye on her.....*Beg your pardon*
- Turn a blind eye and let her pilferage stuff......*Ugh*!!

I looked at my expense book and calculated the additional expense. Well, it was just a little over a thousand bucks. *But that's not the point, how can I expose my kids to an influence like her, someone who steals without any remorse.*

I decided to discuss with Rajan in the evening when I had recovered from the shock of all this! I called up Suman and told her not to come that day. I don't know what I would have done if I had seen her that day, my meditation and resolve for maintaining my cool notwithstanding!

The day went by very quickly; all I could think of was the dooming catastrophe. Even though I tried my level best, this problem refused to leave my mind. I contemplated putting a CCTV covering the kitchen area and show her the footage of her stealing. I could warn her and continue with her then. She may not leave as she did need the work and I was paying her well. Then I remembered Dinesh, a servant our uncle had when we were kids and this option was ruled out….

"Rashi you remember that weirdo?"

"Of course I do, how can I forget!!"

Madness from The Past

(The following narrative is from Rashi, so the "I" is once again Rashi.)

My paternal uncle, Suresh Chacha, had this super-efficient servant called Dinesh, who had been working with him for over two years. Being extremely reliable and willing worker, he was trusted by all in the family. He understood the needs of not just each family member but also the regular guests they had. As we used to spend a large part of our vacations at our uncle's place, and Dinesh took good care of us, we too were attached to him.

"Dinesh Bhaiya…."

"We want to go to the swings. Uncle says we can go only if you accompany us."

"Rashi beta, let me finish the ironing, last few clothes left. We will go then."

"No….o, Bhaiya, we want to go now!! It's going to be dark soon, and then no one will let us stay outside". I would yell, pulling his sleeves.

"Ok... Ok... lets go," saying he'd pick me up and take us out.

Another day…

"Bhaiya what have you prepared for us today?"

"Our two princesses would get their favorite rajma-chawal."

"Wow! Have you made it? I simply love your rajma-chawal. I will eat loads of it and then have a stomach ache, what will you do then?"

"I know you kiddo, I have your Hajmola. And if that doesn't help, I'll make lemon soda drink for you. You'll love it."

Like an elder brother, he would dote on us. My cousin would comment how Dinesh Bhaiya never pampers any of them and was so very prim and proper with them. But I guess it was the familiarity amongst them, and also the fact that they treated him as a servant, whereas we gave him the respect of an elder brother.

The summer of 86 is well etched in my mind. We were at our Suresh uncle's place and our aunt and her kids had started behaving a bit weird. I remember, one day my cousin, in his late teens, who both of us used to hero worship, was moving the bolt of the door up and down mumbling some gibberish. Another day, he was walking up and down the stairs mumbling something like *"I will avenge my death, you cannot get away....I am keeping a close watch on you, don't try anything......"* We had got really scared.

Our Aunt had been having a persistent headache for three consecutive days. Every morning she used to throw up. Not a morsel of food would stay with her. Uncle kept giving her some home-made drinks so that she doesn't get dehydrated. My younger cousin, was telling me what looked like tales; *"there is a worm floating above your head, your eyes are turning cockeyed, I am a fairy, I will turn you into a witch"* ...... Both of us were terrified.

As Uncle was caught up with tending to the three, we would curl up to Dinesh Bhaiya, who would tell us some stories from Mahabharata so as to distract us. Uncle had called two different doctors and neither of them was able to figure out the problem.

Then our grandmother came over. She made her famous kaada; a home-made medicine comprising of various leaves and roots with medicinal powers. It took two days of regular in-take for all three to get cured.

We went back home full of new tales to tell our friends when the school re-opened. It took a good two to three months for us to forget the whole incident. That winter, my uncle moved to another country and he had to let Dinesh go. But since he had been such a wonderful and faithful servant, he recommended Dinesh to my maternal uncle, Manish Uncle; who at that point was looking for a servant.

We were so happy, that now when we would visit Manish uncle, Dinesh Bhaiya could continue to pamper us.

Next summer, we went to stay with Manish uncle for a week. I usually did not stay at their place for long, as there were no kids our age. Our only cousin in that house was 10 years my senior and "hated" tinie-minies like us! He thought we were a nuisance as uncle would not let his friends stay over late when we were at their place. My aunt, though, was extremely fond of us and would leave no opportunity to pamper us and my grandmother used to dote on us. Both of them would make delicious food for us, take us for theatre and movies, shop for us, etc.

Yet, lack of company did not make that place our favorite house to spend our vacations. This year however, we were looking forward to going there as Dinesh Bhaiya was there.

"Astha, I don't know what's happening!!"

"*Once again the pillion seat of my bike has been slashed in the centre*!!" cried my Uncle

"Manish, I think we should report this to the police. This is the third time in a week when someone has slashed that seat!"

"What I don't understand is, what is this person gaining by troubling us! And what do I complain about? It doesn't seem to make any sense."

It was a strange occurrence that was happening at our uncle's residence. Many of his neighbors used to have their bikes parked next to his, but for some strange reason, someone was slashing through his seat only. They did call in the police, who after some questioning left to go back clueless. However, a visit by the police deterred the culprit and this strange occurrence stopped taking place. Another story for our school friends! *Wow, our summer vacations seem to have become dramatic these last few years!!*

The rest of the stay was uneventful.

About six months later, one day when we returned from school, we saw our parents in a very intense discussion.

"Hello Papa, how are you home so early today? Are we going somewhere? Is there some occasion?"

"Hold on dear, we are not going anywhere, we have just returned from the hospital."

"Oh! What happened?" I asked worriedly.

"Vijaya Mausi (our mother's sister) is admitted to the hospital as she had food poisoning."

"Oh how is she? What did she eat? Did she eat out?"

"Actually, she was at your Manish Uncle's place and the police think she has been drugged by Dinesh and so they have taken him in custody."

"Dinesh Bhaiya!! That's impossible! He is such a wonderful person," I started crying.

"Please calm down Rashi! I know this has come as shock. Had forgotten how attached you are to him. But let me tell you what has been going on at Manish uncle's place since a couple of months. Your uncle, aunty and cousin had not been not keeping well, had been behaving odd. Uncle was getting paranoid that someone was stalking him, Aunty was hallucinating; imagining all types of catastrophes befalling her family, and your cousin had been throwing up every now and then."

We were stunned. That reminded us of the time we had spent at Suresh uncle's house. Then we recollected, Dinesh Bhaiya had been there too when such things were happening there.

Very hesitantly, I enquired; *"Was Dinesh Bhaiya behind it?"*

"Yes dear, they did not realize it until yesterday, when your Vijaya Mausi visited them and after having dinner, started throwing up pretty badly. They rushed her to the hospital, where the doctors had to drain out her stomach. As the contents of her stomach were tested, they found a local drug called 'dhatura' in it. That's when they called the police. When the police learnt of all that was happening in the family, they got suspicious and started questioning Dinesh. He admitted to his crime. He had been giving this drug to the entire family, except your grandmother, for two months and had been increasing the quantity steadily. So, the drug, though was causing some adverse reactions, had not poisoned them. Since Vijaya Mausi was given a large dose all of a sudden, she had poisoning and so, Dinesh got caught."

"Why? Why did he do this? They all treated him like a family member."

"It was due to some belief he had. His mother has been keeping unwell and some 'tantric' had told him if he does all that, she would get well."

"Papa, I think he had done the same earlier as well."

"Yes darling, he had. In fact, he had been to some other mischief before this, at your uncle's place. Remember, you told us how someone used to slash his bike's seat. Well Dinesh used to do that as well. That time it was for his brother's college result."

"But I don't understand, how causing harm to anyone would bring health to his mother. It's so illogical!"

"There are these stupid superstitions that some communities hold. It's kind of mental illness. Unfortunately, till our country folks are educated well, we cannot get rid of these superstitions. Many people have lost their lives due to such madness."

"Yes Papa, we read in our history class how heads of animals and even human beings were offered to please so called Gods of different communities. We thought these were things of past, but looks like such stupidity still exists."

That incident had left a very deep scar on both me and my sister's psyche. It took me a long time to start trusting people, especially the 'bhaiyas' and the 'didis' employed at various households. But somehow, what stayed with Preeti was this fear from anyone external preparing her food. It was only when she had kids and managing home, office and kids became a challenge that she started using domestic help to cook food, but then, she made sure that the cook ate from the same preparation that was served to her family.

However, some fear associated with Dinesh's incident stayed with Preeti. It had ruled out the option of keeping Suman after a confrontation. So either, she could confront Suman, and throw her out; or she would need to create circumstances that would prevent Suman from stealing.

That evening she had reached home feeling totally drained. She had ordered some pizza-pasta meals for the kids and herself. For Rajan, she had prepared some rice and pulses as he was yearning for home cooked food after a long tour. She didn't want to spring on him this problem as soon as he arrived, so she waited well after the dinner. But her countenance must have revealed her tension, as a couple of times during the evening he enquired if everything was fine.

As they sipped their late night coffee, she brought him up to date on the home front. She had resigned herself to the possibility of being without a cook in sometime. She shared with him the options she had evaluated and why she thought none of them were feasible.

"I think the best option is she comes later in the evening; say 7:30 PM when either you or I am home."

"But why would she agree?"

"Pay her extra."

"What?"

"Pay her a slight premium if she is willing to come later."

"Wow! That's a great idea!! She wouldn't know that I have realized she is stealing, and I can also keep an eye for any other mischief she tries!"

With this big problem being resolved, well almost resolved, she had a perfectly deep sleep that night. The next day, for a premium of a couple of hundreds, Suman agreed to the new timing.

So Suman had continued for the last one year but then her mother-in-law fell ill and Suman had to leave town for a few months. Muniya's term had also ended.

Preeti had employed the weird girl and lecherous cook around the same time and fired them together. Now my sister had neither a maid nor a cook and guests were expected soon.

I realized my sister fared no better. In fact, she was in a worse situation than me.

Finally a Maid without Cell-Phone

I resolved to keep a maid that will not have access to cell phone during her time at my place. I also made it a point to hide all my personal programs till last minute from these maids.

This is when Roma came in our lives, I remember the first day with her. She seemed to be crazy about nail art and it looked like she would be spending some good amount of time on it. But for me if she was willing to work diligently, this harmless activity was not an issue. Besides, she had reluctantly agreed to not keeping a cell phone.

Though, she was a sweet girl who had fairly decent skin tone, I soon realized that she seemed to have a beauty fetish and was determined to make her skin turn white, by using generous portions of various fairness creams. I tried to talk her out of this as I feared she could contract some skin infections, but my advice fell to deaf ears.

Anyway, like always, I had seen her entry as a beginning of a new chapter in my life

The new day began, with a new ray of hope.......my life is back on track....touch wood!

Of course there would be the initial few days of effort of training the new girl but that's a small price to pay. Getting up at 6 AM that day was no challenge at all; there was that undisputed lightness in my steps and my head. And guess what awaited me?

There she was, in the kitchen, making tea for us!! I could not believe my eyes….this must be a dream…after all this was her first day! How did she find her way around? "*Roma*", I stammered. *"How come you are up so early on your own? How did you know the time?"*

She smiled sweetly and retorted, *"Namaste Madam, I know you got me here for your comfort. I don't need you to wake me up. You had mentioned about your schedule last evening and so had set an alarm in the clock that was in this room. You don't worry about the morning chores. Let me know what needs to be made by what time and you would have everything ready."*

I looked on with stunned silence, and before I could utter a word, she continued; "*Madam, I assume you would like me to finish the kitchen work before starting any other activity?"* I nodded with intense delight.

I came with delicious looking tea to our room and woke up Sameer. Still I could not get my voice back. Sameer was getting really concerned;

"Rashi are you fine? Is everything ok? By now Sameer was fully awake; he genuinely thought there was trouble in the morning. That's when I got back to my senses; I hugged him with tears of joy flowing down my eyes.

"*Darling, can you believe this tea was made by Roma*?"

"Roma who," came the blank look.

"Our maid Sameer, our precious maid! She got up at 4:30 on her own and has made this tea before I got into the kitchen."

Sameer smiled realizing he can look forward to heavenly home for the next few days!

For me, it was a dream come true! Not only did the tea turn out to be excellent, Roma had prepared the entire breakfast and packed our respective lunches. My derailed life was getting back on track.

In the evenings, I would call her just as I was about to reach and she would have hot tea ready for me before I could put my bags down. Having spent the whole day alone or in company of kids, she would have multiple tales to tell, which I would listen (or appear to listen) patiently, as I glanced through my personal mail and WhatsApp messages. When I learnt that she could also cook well, I spoke to Sajida asking her to take charge of cleaning the house instead of cooking our lunch.

Roma's cooking was phenomenal. We no longer had to go out for Chinese or Continental as she made them as good as a qualified Chef.

A couple of months passed blissfully. My house was maintained with professional precision and the kids had also got very fond of Roma Didi. The contentment of home got spilled over to the office and my productivity increased manifold. It was as if the days had expanded and I could accomplish a lot more in a day.

But alas! When things are too good to be true, they usually are. While going through my bills, I noticed that our landline phone bills had started going northwards. I first checked with kids and hubby and all of them seemed to be using their mobile phones. Then I confronted Roma. She admitted to having used the phone once in a while.

I politely told her that in case she wants to call, she can do it with permission and she readily agreed so I thought the matter had ended. But due to the last two incidents, I had got CCTV cameras installed in my house and I checked them regularly for the coverage. Snooping is also a time consuming activity…phew!

During one of the CCTV recordings, I noticed that she was spending way too much time in the balcony. When I confronted her, she broke down and admitted that she had been using phone in the balcony. I was stunned. She had pleaded with Sajida to buy her a mobile phone, and as she knew that I am keeping a watch on her, she had been using her phone in the balcony. I confronted Sajida too, who confirmed.

That day I realized that technology cannot be stopped; hence the best way was to accept it and move on.

The Park Rendezvous

*"**M**adam, can I take Muskan to the park in the evening? She will make new friends and can play there too."*

"What a nice suggestion, Roma, by all means, please do." Muskan was also keen to go, hence I gave the permission. And then, she became extremely regular in her visits to the park.

One day, when I was working from home, I noticed that she took around half an hour to get dressed and ready to go to the park. Now this was strange as I thought going to the park was meant to be more of an excursion for Muskan than for Roma.

I temporarily halted my work, put on my nondescript guise and started to follow them. On the way, I met Mrs. Satija and my cover was blown.

"Oh Hi Rashi, how are you, haven't seen you for a long time...."

"Hello, Mrs. Satija, am doing well, how are you?"

"I am fine. How are things? I don't see you these days, but I see a lot of your maid and your daughter Muskan during my daily walks to the garden."

Hmm...maybe I need to encourage her to speak and pump her for some information, I thought. But Mrs. Satija didn't need any encouragement.

"Oh really!"

"Yes, I see them every day, in the park, with a lot of kids. They are enjoying themselves."

Thank God! At least Muskan was having a good time, but before I could rest my fears, came the interesting bit.

"Rashi, your maid seems to be spending quite a lot of time with her friends these days. Sometimes, they leave the kids with some younger girls and then start to chat with the boys and the men around. I heard through one of the maids that they are planning a wild party for the weekend."

"I have also noticed Roma with one particular person, for the past few days. I am afraid some romantic liaison is on. Anyway, thought I should share this with you. Chalo, I've got to go, I see Mrs. Duggal, need to catch up with her too."

I froze in my tracks; this was interesting and potentially dangerous. Now the dilemma was that Muskan was safe and she was also enjoying the park, but Roma was supposed to keep an eye out for her. Also, I had experienced and borne the brunt of these so called "fun" relationships.

Confront or Leave? What is it going to be?

"Roma, what is going on?"

"Madam, what do you mean?"

"I mean exactly what is going on in the park with that tall gentleman?"

"What gentleman, madam?"

"I see that you leave Muskan with someone else and walk off with some tall guy."

"Madam, I always keep Muskan in sight, no matter where we go or sit." She sidestepped the question.

"Roma, whatever you have with that gentleman is your personal business; I want to make one thing clear that you will not do anything when you are working. After working hours, you can do whatever you want and I would have nothing to interfere, hope this is clear."

"Yes Madam...."

With this, this dangerous chapter ended and I took a sigh of relief. I started the practice of coming home unexpectedly so as to remove the comfort of knowing a safe time. In fact, as Sameer's office was nearer to home, I requested him to do surprise home visits once in a while. Roma had indeed stopped meeting any guys during working hours.

Maid Gone!! Too Much Work, Rat Attack

*"**H**oney, I'm home! Hey Rashi, what's the matter? You do not look too good?*

"The house also seems quieter today. Roma...Roma.....where is she?"

"Roma is gone!!"

"What do you mean gone?"

"Yes, gone, she packed some things and left?"

"Oh!"

"She said there is too much work in this household."

"What??"

"Yes, the dishes are dirty, the house is not cleaned up, I don't know what to do...."

"Okay...."

"What do you mean, Okay??? Is this Okay???"

"No...no, I was just trying to assess the situation...."

"Sameer, there is no time to think for God sake, we need to act. Sameer, please do the dishes.... And MEHAK, MUSKAN..., please pick up your clothes and shoes and put them in the cleaning basket, they are filthy..."

"So what really happened Rashi, was she asking for a raise for more work, I mean we could work this out.....I mean nobody walks out without giving some notice....."

This is not happening....what a beginning to a Saturday evening...... the thought kept drumming in my head

"Sameer, are the dishes done????"

"Oh just on it honey...will take some time, am an amateur not a professional....."

"DO YOU THINK I AM A PROFESSIONAL DOING THE LAUNDRY?????"

"Oh no, Honey, just blabbering..."

What a sight! Formally dressed, tie and sleeves rolled up, washing the dishes, all wetty and sweaty.

"Papa, can I click your pic? Have never seen you like this before..........," someone seems to be having fun!

"My back aches.....my shoulders pain......I need some painkillers to survive, by the way what happened?"

"Me too Sameer, along with all this, my head too is about to burst. Look, lets cancel tonight's movie tickets and dinner reservations, we will order dinner at home. There is too much work in the house and I am too tired, and in no mood, to dress up. Now be a sport and order some food for the evening, make sure to have veggies in it, not just some junk. Also...."

Sameer duly obeyed and managed to keep himself safely out of sight and reach, till the night. Once the kids were asleep, he calmly asked, "*What happened Rashi?*"

I told Sameer that this had been going on for some days and the final straw came that day. Since the time our neighbor, Tanya, had got a new maid, Roma had been restless. She had started pestering me for a raise, as she thought that Tanya's new maid was being paid more. She was forever on the balcony chatting away to glory with Tanya's maid. I had checked with Tanya, but she denied of having raised the market rates. So I realized that her maid was just playing games with Roma, and tried to explain the same to her but to no avail. Her fidgeting had started with…

"Madam, I have pain if I bend too much, hence I cannot pick things up from the floors."

So I gave Roma some painkillers and ointment, which she finished in no time but still she claimed of no respite. I then took her to a doctor, who ordered some blood tests and prescribed some more medicines. All reports were fine but the pain would not go away.

The other day, I was doing some work when I saw a dirty area near the fridge and pointed it out to Roma. Just then I saw a rat and jumped a foot high! Immediately, I called up the pest control agency whom we engage every quarter and asked them to send someone ASAP. Roma remained unperturbed by it all, claiming that she has too much work to do.

Now during Roma's afternoon nap near the fridge, one of the rats managed to bite her. She woke up with a start and created such a ruckus, all hell broke loose. I tried to pacify her and understand what had happened but was humiliatingly unsuccessful. She huffed and puffed and stormed out of the house saying not only is she paid less, she is unsafe in this house, is shown no respect etc. etc. I have been trying to reach her but she is not even answering her phone now. She said that she is overburdened with work and doesn't want to stay here anymore.

"So ends my story for the day, Sameer, and in this year of the rat, as the Chinese fortune cookie calls it, we are in for trying times....please be so kind to set up the alarm for tomorrow's ordeal to begin."

Postscript: The pest control guys arrived; put the rat traps (managed to catch three rats) and cleaned the house, another two weeks of misery followed by new hope and new beginning.

Manna from Heaven

It had been two weeks since the last episode, I was already exhausted. To cheer myself up, I called Preeti, but she was travelling. Then I called up my cousin who somehow always had had great luck with domestic help.

"Hi Anju, how are you?"

"Am fine, long time Rashi!"

"Yeah, I have been quite busy in the last few weeks."

"Oh really? Why?"

"No marks for guessing..."

"Maids again?"

"Yes, how are things at your end?"

"Rashi, can we talk about something else? I am a little superstitious when it comes to this topic.

I have a good going till now and don't want to spoil this. I am keeping my fingers crossed since the last few years. Fortunately, maids in this part of the country are more professional. We too are completely dependent on them. My son is so fond of his didi that he prefers to go with her to the park than anyone else. Sometimes, you can get lucky, I guess. Here, they are reliable and would refuse if they don't want to or cannot do any work. The only drawback is they are inflexible about their time so if you have guests and want them to stay late or come early, they would simply refuse. And of course, informing in advance to take a day off is absolutely below their dignity. But as of now, I am not complaining."

"Wow, sis, you must have some good karma in your past life to deserve this. But why are no full time maids available in your city."

"Rashi, the ones who are wanting to be a full timer, typically migrate to larger cities. They get better money and better living conditions there."

"Hey Anju, do you know anyone who may be wanting to move now? It would be great if I can get someone like that."

"Sure, let me check and I will get back."

Finally with the help of my cousin I was able to get a live-in maid; without even having to pay for the agency commission!! It's sad how the commission sometimes is more than what gets paid to these poor women who work day and night! So, to be honest with self and my conscience, the salary I decided for her was approximately what my payout would have been in case I had taken the maid from an agency.

Jewelry Missing

*"**R**ashi, my necklace is missing!"*

"It can't be....Please check..."

"No it was here yesterday....."

Sameer's Aunt had just arrived from UK and as she had some work in Delhi, she had decided to stay with us. I was not too fond of her as Aunt Maya had a penchant for creating dramas. She was quite wealthy or so she would like all of us to believe and simply loved to flaunt her jewelry. Hence, the theft, came as no surprise but unfortunately it happened in my house with disastrous consequences.

"Can you check with your Maid, she must have taken it...?"

"Aunty, she has been with us for quite some time and is totally trustworthy. I am sure you must have kept it somewhere and forgotten about it?"

"No.... No..., I remember coming back home from Mr. Mehta's party and had taken off the necklace, and kept it on the table, now I cannot find it. This necklace was given to me by your uncle and he had bought it from Tiffany's, it is extremely valuable and extremely dear to me for emotional reasons. It is one of my most expensive pieces, and my entire set will get spoilt if I lose it."

"Where did you keep it, Aunty?"

Oh I don't remember; maybe on this table or the other, oh I am so stressed?"

Now our house has one main entrance and one side entrance. On the main entrance, there is table, which also doubles up as a shoe rack. Normally we keep things there, which are of daily use and less value. Next to it are the sofas and the side tables. This is where things that are slightly more expensive and showpieces are kept. Adjoining it is the dining table and though it is meant predominantly for food, but with teenagers in the house, you can find pretty much everything strewn all over it. Once in a while, when I lose my cool, the kids clean it up in no time.

"You know Rashi how careful I am (Oh really!!). Can you please ask her?"

"Aunty, have you checked your bags? Are you sure about it? Aunty, this is a grave accusation, it can have serious consequences."

"Rashi, I have checked and am quite sure, I kept it here. Please ask her."

I believe it is a bias that the moment something goes missing, people believe it must be the hired help, so I had to be sure before I asked Sunita.

I hate it when people are careless with their things and then go about accusing poor people of stealing. I wanted to thoroughly check the entire house before any further action. I went and looked at every nook and corner of the house but the necklace indeed was missing. In fact, I had Aunty check her bags once again in my presence, just in case she had missed it. By now, I was worried and didn't know how to ask Sunita without her taking an offense. She is such a lively caring girl and I am fond of her. I checked with the kids, if they had seen the necklace but they too had no clue.

I asked Sameer's advice on whether I should ask Sunita. Though he too didn't like the idea but questioned what options we had! Hence I popped 'THE QUESTION'.

"Sunita, do you remember Aunty's necklace."

"Yes, Madam"

"Do you have any idea, where it is?"

"No Madam"

"Sunita, I believe you, but since the necklace is extremely valuable, we are going to report this to the police."

"No, Madam, please do not do this, they will suspect me and take me for questioning."

"Sunita, nothing will happen, I will be with you for all the time."

But I could see that she was not so sure.

To make things worse, Aunty was getting impatient;

"Rashi, please call the police, the truth will come out. After all with all your police connections, from your last trip, you can at least ask for help."

So I called up the beat policeman who had come over for Mamta's investigation to look into the matter.

Surprisingly, he arrived immediately. Officer Chauhan, was very smartly dressed and was very curt. He asked the usual questions like, *when was it last seen? How did it look like? How much was it worth? People who visited the house during that time* etc. He questioned each of us individually and together including Sunita. He did not overly bother Sunita, besides asking her to be available for questioning later.

I suddenly remembered that we had CCTV footage of the house. I had installed the CCTV after the incident with Shanti. We had spent quite some time researching for the ideal solution and we had had this customized. It had helped us in the past with Roma and I thought this might be useful.

On sharing this information, police officer Chauhan, face brightened. He immediately took the recordings and said that he will return them later after watching them for clues.

Sunita was visibly terrified so, I tried to pacify her and asked her not to worry but she did not look convinced.

The next day, Sunita refused to come out of her room, she was suffering from high temperature. I decided to take her to the doctor, but Aunty was becoming annoyingly difficult to control.

"My necklace is gone and now Sunita is acting up, I am telling you she has hidden it somewhere or given it to someone, who is probably pawning it off somewhere in the city, maybe it's already sold out. Oh what a mess! I am

cursing myself of coming over to this city, this time for the weddings. I should have stayed back in UK."

I left Sameer to manage at home, Aunty and the kids. Fortunately, it was a weekend, and so he was available to manage the chaos. I took Sunita to the doctor who told me it's psychological and she is extremely scared. I spoke to her reassuringly.

"Sunita, you have been with me for two years now, I trust you completely. That is what I had told the police officer who came yesterday. He didn't ask you too many questions, did he? So why are you so scared?"

"Didi, the sight of police officer scares the shit out of me."

"Why?"

"My father used to work as a supervisor in a factory in Raipur. One day, some of the finished goods got stolen and the blame came onto my father. I know he was innocent as he had not brought any extra money home for last few months before the incident. But still the police took him away. A few weeks later they found the real culprit but by that time my father had lost his job, his reputation and so his will to live. He hanged himself on the tree the day he was released. I can never forget that day..."

And she started sobbing uncontrollably! I was aghast. Because of carelessness of my irritating relative a young girl of 20 has had to undergo so much trauma.....

I told her to cry out her fears to her heart's content, but take my word that no police officer is going to harass her as long as she is with me. I called up Sameer and told him that I am not bringing her back to our house till this thing is sorted out. There was no way I would make her continue to undergo the trauma. I narrated to him the complete story of poor Sunita, and he too was contrite.

I called up Trish, related the entire drama to her and requested if Sunita could stay with her for a couple of days. She had witnessed how a strong bond had developed between Sunita and me, and she also concurred with my judgment that Sunita is not the thief, so she was agreeable to have Sunita stay with her.

I dropped Sunita and rushed to office. As we had our board meeting coming up next week, I had called some of the staff to office and was working that day. Well, to be honest, the presence of a certain undesirable, unwelcome, nuisance of a relative at our home was an added incentive to stay away. I had my breakfast on the way to office. I was feeling queasy and the silence in the office did not help. By the time I had finished going through urgent mails and reached the meeting room for the discussion, I was quite edgy and distracted.

"Rashi, what is your sense on this innovative idea Chitra has come up with?"

"Sorry Tushar, but can you just bounce it off again?"

Now this was embarrassing, I was not fully there in the meeting.

My entire day was spent reminiscing and thinking about this theft, I was indeed worried about the jewelry but frankly speaking, was more worried about Sunita and how all this had affected her. She had been a good help, probably the best I had ever had, and I was so miserable that she was my aunt's prime suspect. Though I knew she was not guilty and truth will prevail but the interim period that drags between being under suspicion and reality emerging must be so agonizing.

Suddenly my phone rang and it was Officer Chauhan! He asked Sameer and me to meet him at a designated place. The area where he had asked us to meet was in the part of the city where we seldom visited; especially after twilight. It was a crammed and dingy area.

As it is almost inaccessible by car, one needs to park outside the area and take a cycle rickshaw. The old orange sodium vapor lights lit the unpalatable street, and one could see a maze of electric poles and wires hanging all over the place.

It feels like a totally different world from where we spend most of our time. Here time seems to stand still. The dusty panes, nails jutting out of the wooden panels, metal bar protruding out of nowhere and seemingly leading nowhere, seemed a little edgy. I gripped Sameer's hand who reassured me not to worry.

There was no one around to give us the parking ticket. A lone rickshaw was available to take us to the destination.

We met the officer along with his fellow mate. They signaled us to follow them on foot as even the rickshaw could not navigate into the by-lanes. The officer took us inside a dingy colony, where the motorcycles and scooters were parked with eerie precision, under dim lights, crisscrossing through the by lanes, along the some kaccha, some pucca houses, with hardly any space and surprisingly no people. Finally we arrived at a pawn shop. I was extremely scared but kept my nerves as Sameer was with me. It was twilight, moving towards darkness, and this was giving me the chills. Officer Chauhan stepped inside, leaving us alone on the street outside.

Even the weather was chilly and I continued to feel uncomfortable, despite having Sameer and the police officers in the vicinity. There was a sudden rush of anxiety. The lonely street, the time of the day and the dim light, all together had a very potent impact on my nerves. After sometime officer Chauhan asked us to come inside. The room was dimly light. However, the dimness of light did not prevent us from immediately noticing what Officer Chauhan wanted to show us "THE NECKLACE". We identified it as our Aunt's and Officer Chauhan took it in his custody. We came out of the lanes and he asked us to accompany him to the police station.

At the station, he filed his report and after reading, we signed the same. On identifying the necklace, we were asked to submit a pledge, which we did and took the necklace back home. We thanked the officer for his field work and requested his presence for a cup of tea.

We finally reached home exhausted and Aunty was overjoyed to see the necklace.

"See I told you, Sunita was at fault, which is the reason she feigned her illness and you like a fool took her to some other house. I am sure, the police would have threatened her in the police station where she would have confessed to the entire episode, leading to the necklace."

I could not take it no more but before I could speak Sameer spoke firmly;

"Don't jump to conclusions!! The only person responsible for this was you. In the CCTV footage that was given to the police, it was clearly visible that you had very carelessly left your necklace at the side table right next to main entrance. It was in clear sight for anyone passing by our door. Unfortunately, not everyone is like Sunita and can resist a temptation so foolishly presented to them."

By now Aunty had been rendered speechless, all her boasting about being a very careful person had been ripped apart and she was listening intently.

"So, day before yesterday when you came back from the party, you had kept not just your necklace but also your purse, which I assume has some currency and your important documents in it. In the morning, you picked up your purse, possibly for your medicine, but did not bother to pick up your necklace. In the afternoon, when you all were sleeping, a construction worker, who is working in the next house, rang the bell and asked for water. Just as Sunita went inside to get the water, he grabbed the necklace, and threw it on the pavement outside. Then he drank his water and probably after the door was closed, he took the necklace from the pavement. He completed his work for the day but next day he reported sick to contractor. He had pawned the necklace at a local shop, who fortunately had it when Officer Chauhan visited him. Police then got hold of the worker, traced him to his house, where he confessed to his crime.

He said he had seen the necklace on the side table in the morning when he came for duty and then when he went out for lunch he saw it again. He realized that possibly no one is aware of this necklace lying over here and so decided to give it a try. So Aunty, your carelessness has converted a simpleton into a thief, and your subsequent drama has caused a young girl to become so fearful that she has fallen ill."

By now, it was very evident that Sameer was fuming. I quietly held his hand, signaling him to control himself. Aunty was extremely shocked by the outburst and must be wondering what has gotten into Sameer. I could see that she was not too remorseful, which is a pity. It is really sad and pains me when someone is falsely accused because of their socio economic background. I wondered how will she hold if she is falsely accused of a wrongdoing and has to face questioning from legal or other authorities.

I called up Trish to check on Sunita, and what she told me broke my heart further.

"Rashi, Sunita has been crying the whole day. She keeps muttering they will take me away."

"Oh God! I am so sorry that she had to endure all this, can you please give the phone to her."

"Sure....Sunita, your Didi wants to speak to you..."

I heard a very soft whisper on the phone.

"Hello, is that you Sunita?"

"Yes Didi..."

"Sunita, first I wanted to tell you that the necklace has been found and thief has been caught."

She started crying and mumbling something…

"Am no thief...treated your house as my house...my family..."

"Sunita, listen to me please. I always knew you had not done it. I am extremely sorry you had to undergo all this at my place. Now, I want you to think for a day and tell me what you would like to do. Would you like to come back? Or would you like to go home to your mother for some time? Or would you like to stay at Trish Didi's place for a couple of days and then come back."

"Didi, I want to go to my mummy. Please send me home for a few days. I promise I will come back."

"Ok Sunita, I will book your tickets for tomorrow and you go home. Now are you happy?"

"Sorry Didi, I will be leaving you like this, but I do not think I can stay here right now."

"I totally understand!"

But did I understand!! I had lost the best help I had ever had, due to one opinionated careless old hag! Sunita had not taken the necklace, I had shown complete trust in her and yet she and I were the two people who were now suffering.

Anyway, the new search began…..

After unsuccessfully trying to get full time maid for almost a month, I once again had to settle for part timers.

The Foreign Sojourn

It was cold, forlorn evening, with the wind blowing furiously. I was waiting alone, on the dimly lit street. I could see a few passers-by, a dog watching in anticipation, with the watchman following behind. Suddenly I was called out from behind…

"Rashi, how much time do we have to wait?"

"Sameer, just a few minutes more."

"Mummy, please when do we leave?"

I called up again and again but there were no answers. I felt like leaving her behind, would serve her right!

It was 10 PM and the girl had still not arrived. I was trying her number but could not reach. Ah….there she is….and not just she alone, a whole village seems to be accompanying her!!

"Munna, can you please take my bag and keep it in the taxi? Please make sure you visit the house every day and clean up the courtyard. Also do not forget to water my plants. You take good care of the house and I will bring some gift for you from there."

"Saya, I was trying your number."

"Madam, I have changed my sim card, now I am carrying the foreign sim card, hence I cannot be contacted on my number. Shall we go now?"

Look at the hurry she was in …

We finally drove off to the airport to catch the flight to Singapore.

It all started when we planned for a vacation to Singapore with one of our friends. Since we were two families, with extremely naughty kids we needed someone to take care of them during the vacation. Now, the question was, who that someone could be! Suddenly Sameer gave a brilliant idea!

"Well, who is your best friend Rashi?"

"Sameer, you expect me to ask my best friend to accompany us to baby sit our kids," aghast I almost screamed.

"Yes, that's what I am saying. Maybe we can take Saya with us."

"Saya!" I frowned.

"Why not? She is familiar not just with our kids but theirs as well, she is efficient and she does understand a little bit of English!"

"Sameer that's a brilliant idea!!" Exclaimed my friend, she continued, *"in fact, both of us can ask our maids, one of them most likely would agree. Whichever one goes, we split the expense."*

Eureka!...... The idea started growing on each of us. The necessary formalities had to follow, like the visa, passports, tickets and the entire bookings. My friends' maid declined, as her kids exams were round the corner and she was also not too keen on travelling far.

Now Saya, was a good, diligent worker, who was living with her parents. She was quite an intelligent girl, but kept to herself, though she did spend a quite a bit of her time on her smart phone. She had been with us for a while and so could be trusted.

"Saya, will you be able to travel with us to Singapore?"

"What Didi?"

I repeated my offer. She said that she will think about it and reply by the end of the week. The week passed uneventfully, and she came back to me with some queries and a few set of requirements.

"Didi, I have no issues and will be happy to go; however, I would like to clarify a few things. I do not have a passport, so you will need to help me with that. Whatever expense that will be incurred on my travel, I cannot bear it. So you will be funding the entire trip. I will also need some pocket money before the trip for the necessary shopping, and an international calling card and data card with international activation for my phone.

I need this money for shopping; you will understand that when I go abroad, I would want to buy some stuff. You know how my salary is used for paying up the loan that my parents had taken for the home, so this extra expense is not possible for me. Didi, you may think I am demanding too much and maybe being a bit unreasonable, but for me it's important. I just cannot afford any additional expense."

Though taken aback by her forthrightness and clarity of thought, I was pretty relieved as most of these expenses we had factored in. She had indeed put her case very professionally and logically. But I did not want to appear as if I'll agree to everything she demands (you need all your negotiation skills, and more, when dealing with the maids), I replied.

"OK Saya, I will discuss it with Sameer and the other family and will get back to you."

We finally made the offer to Saya and she agreed,

- She would get to speak to her mother for 5 minutes every day.
- She will get a daily allowance (in Singapore dollars) in addition to her boarding, lodging etc.
- She will get to go to all the amusement parks with us.
- She will get an overseas calling card with voice and data for her smart phone (one time only, so that she uses it prudently), so that she can WhatsApp and post her pictures on her face book account.

Ah! Getting her passport was another long story……She had to get her voters card, a letter from the village head validating that she was a resident of that village. Luckily, her previous employer had opened her bank account and her salary used to get deposited there. This bank account and her Aadhar card, which she already had, accelerated the process of getting the necessary documents. Finally, since her police verification had been done at the time of employing her, the police verification formality for passport issue was also completed smoothly

After the trip, we came back extremely happy. Saya had been very professional and had excelled in every department. She had even managed to form friendships with the local Filipino maids in Singapore and she had gone out with them once. I was on my edge till the time she had not arrived back, as I felt responsible for her, but she had managed all right. Little did I realize the hazard this would turn out to be….

She had become a local celebrity, with her folks and well-wishers commenting on her photos on Facebook and personally coming to meet her. She asked for the weekend off after arrival as she had bought gifts for all her friends and family. A lot of people were flocking her for advice on the passports and their vacation planning, which she magnanimously obliged.

My friends were also singing high praises of her and she had indeed been extremely helpful, but our elation was short-lived.

"Didi, I would not be coming from next week."

"Why? What is the matter, Saya."

"Didi, I am getting engaged this week. You see, since I have already travelled abroad, people in my community started defaming me and so my parents want to get me married quickly. I am also moving to the suburbs, where I have already got a job with some foreign couple who work with the embassy. They have promised to help me learn English. The salary they have offered is fantastic!

Didi, while in Singapore, I made friends with the Filipino maids there. They are very professional and get exclusive time offs and tickets back to their home country. I also learnt that they are paid extremely well. In Hong Kong, they have exclusive days for maid population on some weekends, where restaurants carry special deals and offers for them. The entire population of maids is out on the streets enjoying and partying. Now that I have a passport, in case I am able to work with the foreign couple for a long time, I can go with them to their country. So am starting with them next week." I was left speechless.

Sonu Bhai Motor Chali-Pum-Pum-Pum

It was a cold Saturday morning, I was snuggled in the blanket, longing for a cup of freshly brewed tea.....anxiously waiting for her to turn up. *No sign, should I call her. No wait, control your anxiety, you are not so dependent on her that you need to call her up every time she is late by a few minutes! Give her some space, don't you get bugged if your boss calls you when you are late by a few minutes! She would be coming soon, if she wasn't coming she would have send me a message. Also, its Saturday so there is no great hurry to get work done.*

An hour passed and then two, and then when I could take the suspense no longer, I placed the tentative call.

"Hello, Shyama, are you coming today?" I asked tentatively.

"Oh Madam, I could not make it today, had some work at home."

"Oh, but why didn't you call or message?"

"Madam, normally you call up to check, so I thought will tell you when you call. Also for tomorrow, I am not sure, as someone from my village has come over and we might have to go for some shopping and sightseeing tomorrow. You can call me tomorrow morning to check. Okay, bye."

There goes my plan for a relaxed weekend with a two hour spa treatment!! Moreover, Sameer had invited a couple of his relatives this weekend as they were to consult some doctors in the nearby hospital. Thankfully since it was the weekend, and not just Sameer, but also the kids chipped in, we managed to take care of them well and they went back feeling well looked after.

But a bigger challenge awaited us. In all probability, Sameer's uncle would need to get a knee replacement surgery done and they wanted to get it done by the consultant they had visited. So the plan was that he and his wife would stay with us after the surgery. With the uncertainty over maids always looming large in my household, I was a bit worried.

So before they left us, I had a heart to heart with Sameer's aunt. I made it clear that there are days when maids do not turn up and I just leave the work as is, none of us get hassled about a little bit of dirt or unwashed utensils, and typically order food from outside. If the period of absence extends beyond a day, we reach out to a part time maid in the nearby house, pay her some money and get the work done in her free time. I made it clear that I will not be able to take off in case such a situation arises and she would have to be flexible on this. I know it sounds rather rude, but I thought, it's better to make things clear from the beginning rather than managing expectations later on.

Also, as the plan was for them to stay for about a month, we thought that they would need a driver to have mobility and independence. Sameer's friend had recently bought a new car, and had offered his old car to us for the short duration. The interviews for the driver were conducted by Sameer, who thought himself as an authority on the subject. He did have a lot of experience dealing with casual workers. So after checking the license, getting the verification done and taking a test drive, he hired a driver for them.

A few days later as I was walking towards my house, I met Mrs. Satija again. She is a nice cute lady, who prides herself with current knowledge of colony affairs. She is an exercise freak, or so she would like us to believe, and spends at least 2-3 hours in the neighborhood park, where she supposedly exercises for the stated period. Though it is her ears and tongue that seem to be doing most of the exercise after the first fifteen minutes of brisk walking!! She is indeed our very own, most reliable, source of colony news (gossip!!). She always has some really interesting tales to tell, provided you have time (and patience) to listen. As I had taken off that day and was pretty relaxed, I did not put on my headphones on spotting her,

"Oh Rashi, I heard you have employed Sonu as your driver?"

"Yes, why?"

"Oh he was with me till about a year back, didn't he tell you that?"

"No Aunty, I would have definitely checked with you had I known."

Her desire to offload her story was just too palpable for me to ignore. As expected, the gossip war-chest opened and she started....

"Well, though his driving was good, and he knew most routes in Delhi, but he is an extremely notorious fellow in this neighborhood."

"Oh, why is that?"

"Though he has a wife and kids at his native place, he has number of liaisons with these young maids! In fact, if the gossip mill is to be believed he has been sleeping with a couple of them!"

Now this got my attention! The risk of maid and driver liaison was the very reason I had never kept a driver. And the first driver I employ, turns out to be a Casanova!

"Aunty, is that the reason you turned him out?" I could not resist asking.

"One day a girl came to my house complaining about him. She accused him of cheating her into sleeping with him by promising marriage. But when a new girl came in the neighborhood, his interest waned and he left her. I was shocked and the next day I confronted him. He told me it was none of my business and simply walked out on me. Anyway, good riddance... You be careful Rashi."

Suddenly, I was very uncomfortable. I mean Sonu seemed to be a decent fellow. He had always been respectful and Sameer's relatives were very happy with him. Maybe he has changed, or the girl may have been exaggerating. I recalled the incident at Preeti's house, so couldn't completely trust the girl. So I decided that till someone came to me directly, I would let it rest. But I shared the story with Sameer. Once again the practical, sensible reply came…

"Rashi, what he does in his personal time is his private life. We are not giving him access to our kids or anything of

the sort. Just make sure he doesn't interact with Shyama. Uncle and Aunty are ok with him and most importantly he is temporary, so let's drop it!"

Sonu was a tall thin dark fellow, whose main assignment was to make sure that uncle was safely transported to and from the hospital, and also take Aunty to the market or anywhere else she wanted to go. Typically, though he had regular hours but since the tasks assigned were neither regular nor too time consuming, he did not have much work to do. So, he seemed pretty happy.

As is typical with most drivers in this country, for the first few days, he was at his absolute best, driving well within the speed limit, following all traffic rules, always rushing to open doors for the passengers etc. But then slowly his driving speed started to accelerate. A couple of times when I was returning from office, I noticed that he was driving the car a little too fast. On checking with uncle, he said that though he drives a little fast, he was okay, so I did not pursue this further.

One Saturday, since Sonu was not doing anything, Sameer took him for his official visits.

Now Sameer's car tours are extremely busy. He travels to the outskirts of the city from one end to the other, meeting people, discussing their issues and does not have a fixed plan for any breaks, including lunch breaks. In fact, in his enthusiasm to get the maximum output from the day, he very frequently forgets to have food. This particular day, since he was not even driving, his passion for completing all the possible tasks on that route was at an all-time high, and so he forgot everything about eating. Now my dear

Sameer is quite used to this type of work schedule, but not Sonu. Hence he sulked right through the return journey.

When he came in the house to hand over the keys, I, the well experienced, helping-hand mood expert, could see clearly that something was amiss and we may be on the verge of losing him! So I asked him if everything was ok. Though at first he was a bit hesitant, but then he stated he was very hurt and cannot take this type of neglect.

"Sir did not even give me time or even asked me for lunch. I have been hungry the whole day."

I was a bit puzzled, with Sameer's meetings typically running into 2-2.5 hours, I was sure that this guy should have had enough time during any of these meetings to have lunch or whatever else he was expecting to have. I did not say anything before checking with Sameer.

"Sameer, did Sonu drive almost the whole day through and did not get time to have lunch? He seemed to be sulking and I sensed that either he'll not turn up for a day or two, or worse may even quit!!"

"What?? This idiot has been loitering away the entire time when I was in meetings. In fact, every time I had to move from one location to another, I had spent good 5-10 minutes trying to trace him. It seems it's below his dignity to wait at the car. Why could he not manage something during those two hour waiting periods!! Honestly the last thing I want to be bothered during official work is whether the driver has had something to eat or not."

I could see Sameer was really furious. I tried to calm him down but Sameer's tirade was not to be contained...

"Wait a minute, this jerk got tea and snacks wherever he went. So I don't think its hunger that was bothering him. I think lunch is an excuse; he is not used to earning his salary! On a typical day, he is busy for at most 2-4 hours and gets paid for 10! So today when he had to work the entire 10 hours he could not take it. And frankly Rashi, I care two hoots if he doesn't turn up tomorrow. With online cab services, we are definitely not dependent on these guys. Uncle and Aunty can take one of the rental cars to the hospital."

I thought, wow, I wish one could get maid service on hire the way one gets transport service on hire! Wouldn't my life and that of my various sisters in maid trap, be so much better off!!

Sonu did not turn up the next day. Sameer called him and told him that if he doesn't show up for work in the next hour he was fired. He promptly turned up in an hour's time!! Once again I thought, ah! If there would ever be a time when we could have this kind of upper hand with our domestic helps.

The Driving Bug

"**R***ashi, Sameer, can you come out?"*

Uncle called us.

"Yes uncle, what is the matter?"

"It seems that Sonu has got into trouble. The police have come over and there is seemingly a scuffle going on."

Both of us rushed out to the place where this was happening. On reaching the site, we saw two smashed up cars and a strange feeling started creeping in. Meanwhile the voices got louder…

"Who will pay for the damage? If you don't know how to drive why the hell are you on the road?" The gentleman who was holding Sonu by the collar was complaining and hitting Sonu, regularly. Now this was unacceptable, I started to move angrily towards the man, when Sameer stopped me.

I was puzzled, Sonu, whatever shortcomings he had, was an expert driver. Besides no one has the right to hit anyone, no matter what. The road near my house was a quiet road, with little or no traffic. Meanwhile the policeman was standing there coolly and watching the proceedings, probably expecting the situation to either calm down or go out of hand before he would step in.

After restraining me, Sameer intervened, separated the two fellows, dispersed the crowd, asked the policeman to step in and asked for the details of the accident.

Meanwhile, I glanced towards our car. It was totally smashed from the front. The entire set of machinery had come out, the bonnet was thrown off and the pipes had started to leak. What a mess! I silently said my prayers, that once again, Sameer's prudence paid off as he had given his own car to the driver, and Sameer himself drove his friend's car.

From the corner of my eye, I saw Shyama, with a scared expression on her face. Before I could figure out what may have happened, I heard the gentleman screaming

"Don't let a novice ever drive a car on the road!"

Novice? Sonu? He must have been driving the car? Or was it Shyama? And just when it had dawned on me, Sonu confessed to the crime.

"Madam, Shyama had been pestering me for quite some time to teach her driving. Today being a quieter day for traffic, I thought I can teach her some stuff. This gentleman came out of nowhere and Shyama panicked, ending up in this situation. I was about to call you but this gentleman was not letting me go."

I just lost it, Sameer came over quickly and held my hand before I created a scene! How well he knows me, and how level headed he is!! He told me quietly we would deal with Sonu and Shyama later, current need was to manage the situation. We managed to convince the police and the gentleman that we will pay for his repairs which were relatively minor to the damage done to our car. After much discussion and apologies, we managed to extricate the two out of this mess, called the crane service and send the car to the service centre for repairs.

I was still fuming. This dimwit was teaching Shyama to drive at our expense, without taking any permission. This was not only illegal, it was grossly negligent and dangerous! Thank God no one was hurt, otherwise this would have become a police case of accident by an unlicensed person. For a moment I thought, it would have served the two of them right!

Anyway, we dismissed both Sonu and Shyama immediately. We knew neither of them were in a position to pay even a percent of the damages. For Uncle and Aunty, we managed with a taxi service till uncle got better and went back to their city.

Interestingly, a girl approached me the next day asking for work. I was a bit skeptical till I realized that Sonu had recently ditched her for Shyama and she had been seething since. She had been around when the accident and its aftermath took place. So she wanted to take Shyama's job. It was her way of getting back on Sonu and Shyama! In fact, she had even offered to find a really good driver for us, but since our requirement was not very intense, we did not pick her up on that offer but I hired her instantly.

Church Factor

*"**M**adam, my aunt is trying to fleece me, she takes all my money and sometimes I have to go without food. Ah! My life is so miserable! I work the whole day so that I can send money to my folks back home, but as I don't know how I can send it directly, she takes it all away saying she will send it!"*

"Don't worry, Pushpa, I will help you. Let me know the name of your village, call up your folks and ask for the nearest bank account and branch. We can ask them to deliver money to your folks. It is very simple these days, you know."

She spoke to her folks in the interiors of the country. They found out the post office branch details and sent us the same. We got her money directly remitted there and she was elated.

It's really sad how some of these poor girls leave their families behind, toil through the days continually through several months, and then these middlemen or middle women fleece them. It felt good to be able to help one such exploited soul!

Once the money reached Pushpa's parents and they confirmed it to her over the phone, she was very happy. She became even more diligent with her work. She did not miss a single day of work and was extremely dedicated.

"Thanks Madam!"

"Not to worry, Pushpa. In case your aunt asks, I will deal with her."

"Madam, can I ask for one more favor?"

"What?"

"This Sunday, I want to go to the church. I have found out in my colony, that the prayers happen during the day, in this church. I have noted the address."

I found no reason to deny her the solace / inner peace that she sought with god. This was indeed good for the soul.

"By all means, Pushpa!"

"Madam, can you drop me to the church, I will come back on my own. Aunty does not want to send me to the church. In my village, we always used to go to the church on Sunday, and the priest used to teach us a lot of things, but here aunty, tells us not to go too far off, and we pray at home."

I was aghast; I mean how one can stop someone from visiting God's abode. Having studied in a convent myself, and attended the mass, I was determined to connect this young soul with god.

"Rashi, I want to come over for a week, I haven't seen Mehak and Muskan for ages now."

"Of course, Mummy, you are always welcome here, you know that! Also, please do bring that namkeen that I love. And mummy can you bring some pickles that you had got last time."

"Yes, beta, tell me if you need anything else. By the way, how is Pushpa coming along?"

"So far so good!"

My mother is a grand old lady, but age, it seems, has gone past her without a whiff of damage to her spirit. She seems always in control and has withered many a storm, which included passing away of her father at a very early age, managing the household with her mother till her brother came of age and then taking on the responsibility of a large family, when she got married. Now a retired professor she is fiercely independent, drives her own car, is a fitness freak, and never misses her yoga. She keeps herself abreast with the latest fashion and page three gossip, while at the same time remains well connected in the community.

Whilst she was a working woman with an active social life, I cannot remember a day when she did not have time for us, when we needed her. I don't recollect her ever losing her cool when our domestic help would not turn up (which happened as frequently as ever) even when she was managing a large household of grandparents, aunts, uncles and cousins. I need to learn some of these tricks from her.

"Sameer, Mummy is coming over."

"Oh, great! Mummy coming over equals to awesome food, happy wife and excited kids!! This time don't keep an eye on what I am eating."

"Sameer! Have you seen your paunch? Another few months like this and you are going to look like a pumpkin!"

"Aw! Rubbish, my diet plan can wait for a few weeks. I promise to exercise some more next week onwards."

"Why next week, why not from today?"

"Leave it darling, I am in a great mood now, don't spoil it with your nagging! Oh by the way, you need to straighten up your house. You know, Mummy can sniff dirt from far away and she likes the house spotlessly clean."

Oh dear! Sameer was right, I had better start on it right away, if she sees a speck of dust or an untidy cupboard, I've had it. She will start rebuking me about my home management skills, which would somehow lead to some of my mistakes from the past, and then the present, and finally connect it all to give a very bleak picture of my future. Mothers! They do have a way of putting things across in a manner that makes you feel downright stupid and propel you to start exerting more.

I took stock of the groceries, after all I couldn't have her raising her eyes towards heaven, just because I forgot to replenish sugar on time. The table covers, bed sheets and all the long used upholstery would need to be replaced. Not to forget stocking up her favorite ice cream, another fetish she has.

"Mehak, Muskan, please clean up your room, grandma is coming over and will stay for next week."

"Yippeeee...I can have my special meal that grandma cooks. I will ask her to cook that special meal at least three times next week."

Am I forgetting something in the euphoria? Oh yes, Pushpa. She needs to be coached well to understand that mummy is from the old school of thought. She can sometimes drive the domestic help crazy. Also Mummy is very perceptive and there is little that can escape her eye. I would like to develop this unrivaled talent sometime. Maybe, in a few decades....

"Pushpa, mummy is coming over next week, I need everything including sheets, covers etc to be spotlessly clean. Let me know if anything needs to be replaced. Check the utensils. I will come and inspect them once I am back from the office."

Meanwhile, Pushpa was very co-operative and happy as I would take her to the church this week end.

"So this is your little Pushpa, how are you my dear? All ready for the prayer meet tomorrow? Yes, Rashi has told me about it. It is good to connect with god, everyone needs it these days. Going to the church or praying at home shouldn't matter. How come your aunt is not supportive? I wonder." Pushpa did not answer, she was already lost in her thoughts, I suppose.

On Sunday I accompanied Pushpa to the church. As I waited, I was impressed by the calm manner that everyone was conducting themselves with. Once the service was over, the contrast outside was amusing. It looked like a noisy colorful festival celebration. A melee of people like Pushpa and her friends, gathered around and eagerly enquired about everyone else. It was like a mini bazaar, with shops and items for regular work and praying. Pushpa was getting some attention as she was visiting this church for the first time, and did she enjoy it! I did not disturb her. After all, who doesn't crave for some moments of glory.

"How was the service?" Mummy asked.

"It was good, Pushpa made some new friends."

"Rashi, have you told this to her aunt?"

"No way, I don't think she would approve."

"I think you should tell her now that she has gone once."

"I don't know Mummy, we need to mind our own business and not poke our noses in hers. What's her issue remains her private matter, why interfere?"

"But, you have already interfered in her private matters by taking her to the church. Now I think, it's only proper to inform her aunt."

"I will do nothing of the sort, Mummy."

"As your wish, I just hope you do not have to regret this silence."

After this, we did not pursue this conversation. I also forgot about it, till as prophesized, it came back to haunt me.

A few weeks later…

Ah a blissful Sunday! All my tasks for the day are done, and I have just managed to lie down to take my weekly afternoon nap. My dreams comprised of an ideal world in an ideal setting. In this make believe world I was lying on a white pearl beach, sipping my favorite Pina Colada, chatting with my friends on WhatsApp and watching the beautiful sunset. The kids were lazing around the place, which was next to the clear blue sea.

Just as I was enjoying my date with heaven, I was rudely woken up by a persistent call from Pushpa's aunt.

"Madam, have you seen Pushpa lately. She has been missing since morning and I am worried now."

"She was fine when she left in the morning to go to the church."

"Church? Since when has she started to go to the church?"

"She has been going since last month. She takes an auto to church every Sunday and from there I believe she goes back home."

"Madam, you never told me that she has been going to church."

"Oh I might have missed it. Anyway, she is a good girl, she will be back soon. Let me know, once she reaches home."

"Okay Madam."

Looks like Pushpa may have decided to spend some additional time at the Church. Do I blame her, the poor child! But just to be on the safer side, I tried calling her up.

No response…..Maybe the phone is on silent. I tried to go back to my lovely dreams, but somehow, I could not get sleep again.

Something was amiss. Pushpa had never wanted her aunt to know that she goes to Church. So how come she has decided to stay late, she would know that there is a chance that her Church sojourns would get exposed. And then why is she not picking up the phone? It being on silent is a possibility but a remote one. Let me try again. No response…. I was beginning to get worried now. I had not received any further call from Pushpa's aunty. I had been calling up Pushpa every hour but there was no answer, even though the phone was ringing.

Next day, there was no sign of Pushpa. My mother, who was visiting us again as Sameer was travelling, started to give me "I told you" looks and I started to feel even worse.

"Mummy, can you stop giving me those looks, please?"

"What looks Rashi, I am just anxious about you, that's all."

Ah, these mothers, without saying a word they say it all. Anyway, as it was a Monday, I had to rush to office. I had already spoken to Sajida, and she would do the main tasks. She knew that I always paid her well when she chipped in during my maid troubles.

I was in a middle of an intense discussion with my team, when I got the long awaited call from Pushpa. Giving my team a 15 minutes break, I immediately stepped out and took the call.

"Madam, I am really sorry that I could not call you earlier. I have this horrible headache. A few of my friends from Church had invited me to a party after the mass and time just seemed to fly by. We did have a blast, but resulted in me over sleeping today. I have just woken up and that too with a very heavy head."

"So Pushpa, where are you now? What did you have?"

"Madam, I just had a few drinks, nothing much. I have decided that I am not going back to my aunt's house anymore. I will move in with my friends. I will now be independent. Only problem is that I would not be able to come to your house anymore as the place that I am moving to is quite far. I am really sorry, I know I will not get a madam like you who is so caring but I have to move out of my aunt's house. Thanks for everything, bye."

"Hey listen Pushpa! I do not want to give personal advice but have you thought through this? I mean, do you really want to do this? Are these friends well known to you? Are you sure they will not push you into any illegal activity?"

"Madam, I have ten siblings at home, living in very horrible conditions. With the responsibility of feeding so many mouths, I doubt I will ever get a chance to enjoy my life. In the village, the weather is good but the life is dull. Here in the city, there are so many options. But my life in city has been miserable due to my aunty. She keeps such a strict watch on me, always pestering me to take up more work, no matter what my health or emotional state is. When I move in with my friends, I will be free, with no one watching over me. Isn't that cool? You have helped me in sending money home. But while visiting the church I have

realized what all I am missing in life. Madam, I also want to enjoy, I want to save for myself, to buy new clothes, watch new movies and most importantly I want to buy a smart phone, I have seen people using it to send photos and all kinds of messages etc. Madam, I think it's time I live my life for myself. Please can you convey to my aunty that I will not be going to her house anymore?"

"And why do you think am I going to do that for you? Please have the guts to talk to your aunt and what you do with your life is you call. I would have advised you against this move, but since you are an adult, I will refrain from it. I am just a bit surprised at this turnaround, that's all. Enjoy your life!!"

She was not coming back… Crash, Boom, Bang!

Once again the search would have to begin. Thank God Sajida is there to chip in for a few days. With a heavy heart I went to my meeting……..

Old World....Thought

Hey who is this? Where am I? In my dreams I had moved into the world of Rajas and Zamindars, the era of royalty and old world charm. There seemed to be a wedding in progress…hey hold it, who is this who is getting married! Oh dear it's me!! It is it my marriage that I am witnessing. It seems I am being decked up and coached at the same time. My mother is telling me certain duties that were expected of me and I seem to be listening rather attentively.

"Listen, Mala, you have to perform your duties to the household and specially Madam."

Madam? Now I am the Madam, here, isn't it?

"Mala, please pay attention, you know you are part of the dowry that is going along with her Royal Highness Chandrika Devi. Take care and do not be overbearing, and don't you dare bring a bad name to her and her family. Also if need be, guide her well, like I have guided you. Now, we have prepared your bags and the procession is waiting. Your salary will come to us directly from the Madam's house, so you don't worry about us. You can come and visit us once a year or whenever Madam chooses to visit her mother's place. Now, I know Madam and you have been the best of friends, but please do not cross your limits and do take care."

Oh dear, so in this set up, I seemed to be the maid! I was in the process of being coached to be the maid of a princess, who was getting married. Anyway, I was now being whisked away in the cart along with her royal highness, with all my family looking longingly.

The cart reached a big old haveli, even bigger than the one we stayed in our Madam's town. It was in the middle of lush green lands, and was gorgeous! As we approached the green lands and the huge royal Haveli, I could feel my heart beat growing stronger. I did not know what the future held for me or for my friend. After a ceremonial welcome of the bride and the bride groom, we were given food as the celebrations in the Haveli commenced. After a couple of hours, we were shown to our rooms. A few more people had come along with Madam and me as part of her coterie, but I considered myself special, as I was a part of her inner circle.

Madam, went to her room in the ladies side of the house, after the pooja and the celebrations were over. I had quickly freshened up so that I could get her room arranged as per her liking. We had grown up together and hence I knew her likes and dislikes on the back of my hand. When she came to her room, I was there for her in case she needed any help.

"Oh, Mala, you are a gem, you have already unpacked my stuff and arranged it so beautifully!!"

I was so thrilled to see her satisfaction. "*You must be tired your highness, shall I massage your feet and hands?"*

"Not now Mala, the first person I want to be touched by now is you know whom..." She winked wickedly!

It took me some time to get adjusted to the rules and regulations of the new house. As we all were diligent and hardworking with a keen ability to learn, we did not face many issues. Life in the help's quarters was rather colorful, you could get plugged into the regular gossip of the household as well as the nearby township.

"Mala, do you know that the old grandma snores so loudly, that no one can sleep in the three adjacent rooms, hence they have kept those empty. She still doesn't know it."

"You know the gardener's daughter ran away to the city with the farmer's son to escape her wicked father and the back breaking work that she had been assigned to at this Haveli. They are planning to send a search party, and have come to the Haveli to take advice from his Highness Kunwar Ranjit Singhji. That is why you hear such a commotion in the main hall."

This was an era when running away from home was the biggest crime a girl could commit. Somehow, one would typically get traced and killed if one left the house on her own and went on to stay within the nearby towns. Only escape for the girls was to go and hide in a larger city, where tracing them would be difficult. But that also meant breaking all ties with the entire family and clan.

So with her running away, her duties fell onto another old timer in the house, whose generic duties were passed on to a rather junior housemaid. The main chores of running a house were basically the same, cleaning, washing, cooking, helping, and babysitting! Times have changed but not the house work. The same old chores have been there for times immemorial. The faster means of transport and communication has changed many of our ways and the time taken for doing things, but the wants of a house hold have remained more or less same.

"Mala, I cannot seem to find my pink sari, can you help me locate it?"

"Sure Madam!"

We searched the entire cupboard and the entire set of upper rooms, but could not locate the sari. Madam was really very upset. There was a party scheduled in the evening and she was supposed to wear the same as instructed by her husband.

The entire staff was put into the search operation but we all searched in vain. I started to panic as her clothes were my responsibility. She hadn't mentioned anything but I could see she was miserable and I felt extremely guilty. Suddenly, I heard a faint tap on my door.

"Mala didi, look what I found," I saw a small 9 year old child, carrying THE pink sari.

"Didi, I found this near the mango orchard, where someone must have left the sari, to pick up a mango. So I had picked it up and when Amma saw it, she told me to rush to the Haveli and give it to you."

I was overwhelmed with relief. As my joy knew no bounds, I quickly gave him some sweets that Madam had got for me from England. I quickly inspected the sari and barring a few creases, it was intact. Ironing it well, I presented it to Madam, along with the entire story.

She was able to wear it that that evening and was really exhilarated. Somehow, the story of her missing sari became the talk of the party and I was suitably rewarded and appreciated after the party.

"Mala, can you pack your belongings?"

"Why madam, is there something wrong? Have I done anything to upset you?"

"Oh no Mala, you are my lucky charm!! My husband is moving to a big city as he has been selected in a large university and we have to move with his highness."

"Oh wow!"

Oh how exciting! I had never seen a big city. I quickly completed all the packing and soon we were in the cart. As I waited for the cart to pull us to the nearest railway station, I started feeling a bit nervous as well.

"Wow Madam, it's such an enormous train!" I exclaimed.

It was indeed a very big train, with the steam engine pulling the carts along on a track, much faster than the bullock or the horse. We were bundled in the compartment with other ladies as our luggage was being hauled up in another carriage. The train journey was fantastic and the view from the window was magnificent, with the lush green fields and the trees, in their full glory as it was just after the rains.

City life was interesting. It had so many roads and modes of transport. In my village, everyone commuted by bullock cart or on horses. Here they had cycles, cars, trams and what not. The house where we stayed was smaller than the haveli. It was an old building with slatted windows but it did not have a good ventilation system that made the heat unbearable.

One of the days, as I was returning home after buying some groceries, I entered the street next to ours by mistake. There I saw some kids studying and discussing something quite intently. I went and stood staring at them. A teacher was passing by and she asked me if I wanted to study. I replied in affirmative and then with my Madam's permission and support I started to devote some time to my studies. Slowly and steadily I started to learn the alphabets, sentences and numbers.

Meanwhile, due to the gratitude I felt for madam, I exerted myself to excel in all the household chores and had become quite good at cooking. Soon, Madam's friends started requesting Madam to send me to their houses for cooking when they had parties. At one such party, someone handed me their card and address.

"Mala, if you want to start your own catering or a sweet shop, let me know. I can help you. You are very good." I thought about it for a while and then told Madam about it. She encouraged me to go and find out about it. The house was much bigger than our city house and I was ushered in.

"Welcome Mala", my host appeared, *"I thought you will not come."*

"Madam, I thought, is it possible?"

"Mala, it is quite possible, as I help young ladies get on their feet but you will have to leave your Madam's house. You will have to cut all ties from the past, so do think about it very carefully."

This was not something that I needed time to think about. I told her no at once. There is no way I could betray the love and trust that Madam had ushered on me. I am not an ungrateful brat like Pushpa.

Ah, the moment Pushpa's thought came, my dream was broken and I woke up with a start.....

Maid Saga Continues

Two weeks had passed without a maid, I had come to terms with the reality that I may have to continue like this for some more time.

Then, I got the call.

"Madam, a few girls have come today, what time can you come and take one of them. Three of them are as per your requirements".

I jumped with joy, controlling my squeal of victory. Confirming my intent to take the maid the same day, I called up my husband and requested him to reach the designated place. It was 14th Feb, and Sameer knew this is the best Valentine Day's gift he could get for me.

Suddenly I remembered that I had an important meeting at work that I couldn't avoid, yet this maid acquisition was too important to be delayed by another day. I called up Sameer and asked him to take his mother along to the agent.

Luckily the girl they picked stayed with me for over two years, which was indeed a long duration given by today's standards. Maybe it's lucky for me to have someone else choose the girl for me.

It is interesting how, over the years, the dependence and affordability of maids and other domestic help has been growing, whereas the availability is ever shrinking.

World is a medley of people with their own set of aspirations, dreams, thresholds and needs from life. As long as one is able to contribute to each other's life in some way or the other, one remains connected as though by an invisible thread. However, once that connect breaks, either by some harsh words, crossing someone else's thresholds, the interest is lost and then one gets enough and more chances to rebuild it with someone else.

By this process of life, one collects experiences and they seem to influence one in the way one forms judgments and take decisions in the remaining journey of life.

With domestic help, it is no different. We, the burgeoning middle class, are brought together with these maids due to our need and theirs. During the process, we interact and influence each other in many ways. Hopefully they learn from us, as we do from them. Our paths have crossed as though by destiny, and this connect has stayed for the period destined.

As our stepping stones in this journey of life, each stone has a different story and a past life waiting to be told and explored. The aspirations are sometimes met through this journey, sometimes not, but life is all about making those choices, running after them, hopefully making the process enjoyable, and then laugh over them at a later day. Right now, I am in a mood to contemplate and reminisce, I wonder how long I will be like this, before the next batch of interviewees arrives. Till then.....

Hasta la vista, baby!

This was my maid-en story....

Hope your maid was in today and you could read it in peace......

Dear Reader,

Am sure you would have your own unique maid stories; share them here or maybe with me at maidlessinindia@gmail.com and/or the facebook page Maidless In India